Making
Metal Clay
Jewelry

Making Metal Clay Jewelry

Cindy Thomas Pankopf

KALMBACH BOOKS

Kalmbach Books
21027 Crossroads Circle
Waukesha, Wisconsin 53186
www.Kalmbach.com/Books

© 2011 Cindy Thomas Pankopf
All rights reserved. Except for brief excerpts for review, this book may not be reproduced in part or in whole by electronic means or otherwise without written permission of the publisher.

Photography of finished jewelry projects by Kalmbach Books. All other photography by the author.

The designs in *Making Metal Clay Jewelry* are copyrighted. Please use them for your education and personal enjoyment only. They may not be taught or sold without permission.

Please follow appropriate health and safety measures when working with torches and other equipment. Some general guidelines are presented in this book, but always read and follow manufacturers' instructions.

Published in 2011
15 14 13 12 11   1 2 3 4 5

Manufactured in the United States of America
ISBN: 978-0-87116-431-5

Publisher's Cataloging-in-Publication Data
Pankopf, Cindy Thomas.

   Making metal clay jewelry / Cindy Thomas Pankopf.
   p. : ill. (chiefly col.) ; cm. – (The absolute beginners guide)

"Everything you need to know to get started."–Cover.
ISBN: 978-0-87116-431-5

   1. Jewelry making–Handbooks, manuals, etc.
   2. Art metal-work–Handbooks, manuals, etc. I. Title.

TT212 .P26 2011
745.594/2

Contents

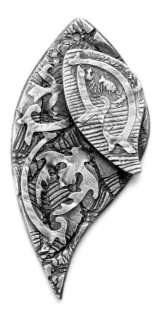

Introduction

THE EASE AND VERSATILITY of working with pure metal in a clay form is wonderful. Metal clay has made making metal jewelry accessible to everyone—you don't need a jeweler's workshop! After gathering some basic supplies, including many common household items, and investing a little time, you'll be able to create fabulous fine silver or pure copper jewelry at home. My goal with this book is to give you the knowledge and confidence to begin exploring this amazing and inspiring medium.

You'll be able to create fabulous
fine silver or pure copper
jewelry at home

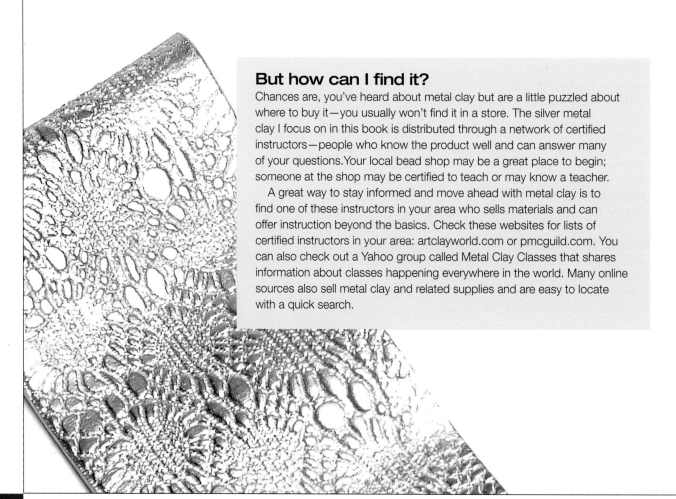

But how can I find it?

Chances are, you've heard about metal clay but are a little puzzled about where to buy it—you usually won't find it in a store. The silver metal clay I focus on in this book is distributed through a network of certified instructors—people who know the product well and can answer many of your questions. Your local bead shop may be a great place to begin; someone at the shop may be certified to teach or may know a teacher.

A great way to stay informed and move ahead with metal clay is to find one of these instructors in your area who sells materials and can offer instruction beyond the basics. Check these websites for lists of certified instructors in your area: artclayworld.com or pmcguild.com. You can also check out a Yahoo group called Metal Clay Classes that shares information about classes happening everywhere in the world. Many online sources also sell metal clay and related supplies and are easy to locate with a quick search.

Basics

Silver clay was the first mass-produced metal clay, and it was the foundation for all other metal clays (which now include bronze, copper, and gold … and the list continues to grow). It's the most reliable and consistent form of metal clay, especially for beginners, and so it's my clay of choice for the projects in this book.

Silver clay is made up of tiny real silver particles with a little bit of water and an organic binder that holds everything together and makes it clay-like. The silver particles are so fine they resemble cake flour.

As you work with the clay, you'll take advantage of its different states. You'll use some techniques only when the clay is wet, and then you'll dry the clay and work with it in other ways. Finally, you will fire the clay. During firing, the binder burns off and the silver particles heat to a temperature that enables them to bond to each other without fully melting. This process is called sintering. It is critical that metal clay is fully sintered or it will be very fragile and could break if you drop it or whack it on a table.

As the binder burns away and the particles pull in and fuse to each other, the clay shrinks anywhere from 9–28%, depending on the brand and variety of clay. For pendants and earrings, the shrinkage won't matter much. But for a ring, the shrinkage rate is enough to make all the difference between the ring fitting perfectly or not at all! (More on this later.)

I designed all of the projects in this book so you can fire them with a simple-to-use, inexpensive, handheld butane torch. It's a great way to get familiar with the firing process. Because all of the pieces are fairly small, they will sinter successfully this way; larger pieces require a kiln.

After you create some of these projects, if you find that you love working with metal clay, then look into purchasing a kiln: You'll be able to fire large pieces and more than one piece at a time. Although torch-firing will work to create small pieces that stand up to light wear, kiln-firing assures a very thorough sinter and creates the strongest possible metal from the clay.

Silver clay = fine silver

After silver clay sinters, it becomes 99.9% pure silver, also known as fine silver. This is different than sterling silver, which is 92.5% silver and 7.5% of another metal, usually copper. This mix of metals, called an alloy, has more strength than silver alone, but is more prone to tarnishing. Sterling silver will develop firescale at the high temperatures, forcing the copper to form unsightly oxides that must be removed by soaking in an acidic solution called pickle. Because silver clay is virtually pure silver, it's very slow to tarnish and none of these treatments are required. That's good news for you!

I know it's tempting to skip ahead and get started on one of the projects. Don't do it! Please read this Basics section before attempting any of the projects. This information will save you lots of frustration and prevent you from wasting clay.

MATERIALS

There are two major brands of silver clay: Art Clay Silver (ACS), which is manufactured by AIDA Chemical Industries, and Precious Metal Clay (PMC), manufactured by Mitsubishi Materials. Both are made in Japan, are very similar, and are readily available in North America and beyond. I think of the two brands like Coke and Pepsi; there are slight differences and people usually have their preference, but ultimately both are cola. With metal clay, despite their similarities, each has its super-secret formula, creating subtle differences that preclude mixing brands.

Types of clay

Lump clay

This is the main material that you'll use for the projects in this book. A package that contains 18–20 grams of lump clay will make about three pendants. (It may be hard to believe that such a tiny piece of clay will do all that, but it really will!)

Paste or slip

Depending on which brand of metal clay you are using, you will find the next product officially called paste (ACS) or slip (PMC). Throughout this book, I'll refer to it as paste. It's simply lump clay with water added to it, presented in a handy jar. It is primarily used to stick lump clay components together. The good news is that one jar of paste can last you for years. As you work, you can add clay dust and tiny bits of scrap lump clay with a bit of water and, voila! More paste! When an entire piece is made up of paste, such as in the "Nature's beauty earrings," you'll use a lot of paste—maybe a whole jar.

Syringe clay

Syringe clay, in its handy little dispenser, contains more water than lump clay but less than the paste. It can be used for anything from caulking to drawing. You should not try to fill your own syringes; this product comes from the factory perfectly smooth and air-bubble free, two invaluable characteristics. Most often you'll use a medium tip—Art Clay's is green and PMC's is pink. Working with syringe clay is a lot like caulking, so you'll often read that I'm asking you to place a "bead" of syringe clay in place.

Paper or sheet clay

ACS Paper Type and PMC Sheet Clay are wondrous materials indeed! Think of them as silver paper. Most things that you could do to a piece of paper, you can do to this type of clay. It does not dry out quickly like the lump clay, so it gives you lots of options. You can create decorative shapes with paper punches, fancy edges with decorative shears, fantastic textures with embossing dies, "fabric" by cutting it into strips and weaving them, and, for folding enthusiasts, silver origami. This type of clay is very thin and easy to melt; the ACS product is a bit thicker than the PMC variety.

Overlay Paste

Overlay Paste is an Art Clay Silver product. It has many uses not covered in this book, such as decorating porcelain or glass (these must be kiln-fired). But it does have other uses. Its different ingredients allow it to bond to slick surfaces or fired silver clay. If a piece was not fired long enough and breaks, Overlay Paste can be applied and the piece refired to mend the break.

Varieties of clay

Art Clay

All Art Clay products are made of 100% reclaimed metals combined with moisture and organic binders. Of all metal clay products, Art Clay products have the least shrinkage.

Standard ACS

This is Art Clay's original silver clay. At the time it was introduced, it was the only silver clay that could be torch-fired because of the tiny size of its silver particles. It is made up of 92% silver and 8% binder and moisture. It is really nice to carve and has a longer working time than its newer sibling, ACS 650. It has 8–10% shrinkage and is available only in lump form.

Standard ACS Slow Dry

Even though this clay is also made up of 92% silver and 8% binder and moisture, a different binder ingredient creates the advantage of greater working time. It is a good choice for making snakes (long, thin shapes rolled by hand), using an extruder to form spaghetti-like strands, and braiding. Standard Slow Dry is slower to dry than 650 Slow Dry. It can also be torch- or kiln-fired. It comes only in lump form.

ACS 650

The second-generation Art Clay Silver product is called ACS 650. The 650 refers to the minimum firing schedule of 650° Centigrade (abbreviated to C) for 30 minutes to fully sinter the silver, which translates to 1200°F for 30 minutes.

Because it has a lower firing temperature, you can incorporate other materials like gemstones, wire, or glass without destroying them during the firing process. Even though it does dry out more quickly than the slow-dry formulas, this is the Art Clay product I use most often. It's easy to add a bit more water to create more working time, and ACS 650 can be reconditioned the most of any Art Clay product. Like Standard ACS, it is also torch-fireable. It has a bit less shrinkage (9%). It comes in lump clay, paste, syringe, and as a special product called Overlay Paste.

ACS 650 Slow Dry

Just like the other Art Clay varieties, Art Clay Silver 650 Slow Dry shrinks 8–10%. Its special formula gives you more working time (but not quite as much as Standard ACS Slow Dry). It has all the other wonderful characteristics of ACS 650, except it must be dried using gentle heat; air drying is not recommended. It comes as lump clay only.

Copper clay

Several manufacturers make a copper clay product, but right now the only one that can be torch-fired is Art Clay Copper. This nonprecious (or base) metal is a wonderful alternative to silver clay. It is 90% copper and 10% moisture and binder with a 10% shrinkage rate. To introduce you to this form, I use Art Clay Copper in the final project of the book, a pendant made from copper clay.

MATERIALS

More varieties of clay

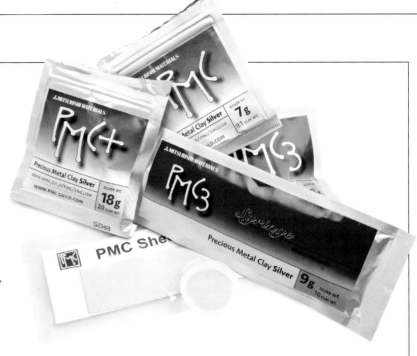

Original PMC

The first metal clay on the market, Original PMC has the most water and binder (about 26%) and the silver particles are of varying sizes. Because of the additional moisture and binder, this variety of clay gives you lots of time to work with it before it dries out. Its high shrinkage rate of about 28% makes details even more intricate, which can enhance a detailed design. It is especially well suited to carving. It is the most porous of all the varieties, making the fired silver very light and not as strong as other types (a knock against a hard object can ding it).

Original PMC must be kiln-fired exclusively (1650°F for two hours), so it can't be used for the firing techniques used in this book. Original PMC is available only as lump clay.

PMC+

Because this second-generation clay can be fired with a torch as well as in a kiln, it really opened up the metal clay world to the casual jewelry crafter. Compared with the original clay, it has a higher concentration of smaller, more evenly sized silver particles and less binder and water (10%), which results in stronger pieces with a lot less shrinkage (about 12%).

Even though it dries more quickly than Original PMC, it has a consistency that's a pleasure to work with. Because of its easy workability, this is the PMC product that I use most and recommend for the projects in this book. PMC+ is available as lump clay, syringe, and sheet.

PMC3

The third generation of the PMC product line is made up of 10% water and binder, just like PMC+. How it differs, though, is that its silver particles are smaller and more evenly shaped, allowing it to sinter at the lowest temperature (1110°F for 30 minutes). It is even stronger than PMC+ and also shrinks about 12%. The texture of PMC3 is very smooth, almost sticky, and dries out the most quickly of the PMC varieties. It can be torch-fired and is available as lump clay, slip, or syringe.

PMC Pro

This is the newest PMC product (as of this writing), and is the strongest of all the silver clays because it's an alloy of fine silver (90%) and copper (10%). It has the longest working time of all the PMC varieties. It must be kiln-fired with special techniques, so don't use this clay with the firing methods described in this book.

Other metals

There are many new metal clays appearing on the market made by several different manufacturers. You can find gold, bronze, other forms of copper—even steel clay. With the exception of gold, these alternative metals are less expensive than silver clay, but all of them require a kiln and a fair amount of experience to master.

If you find you enjoy working with metal clay and want to learn more beyond this book, these new clays will offer exciting challenges for you to explore.

Other materials to use with metal clay

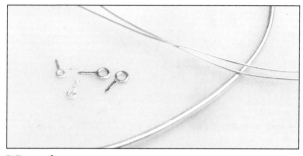

Gemstones

The easiest gemstones to incorporate into metal clay are created in a laboratory—they're known as synthetic gems. Because these stones are lab-grown versions of the real thing, they do not have any of the imperfections that can cause problems when firing natural gemstones. Some good candidates are cubic zirconias (CZs), aquamarine or blue topaz spinel, synthetic alexandrite, and pink or red ruby corundum. Some natural gems can be fired, but play it safe in the beginning by using designated fireable stones. To position the gemstones, a product such as Embellie Gellie, which has its own applicator, is convenient.

Wire and screw eyes

As with prong settings, if you need to incorporate these into wet metal clay, make sure they are made of fine silver—it is 99.9% pure silver just like the clay. Wire can be added to make loops, bails, and decorative elements. Screw eyes are tiny key-shaped findings that can be built into a piece and fired in place to create a small connecting loop.

Fine-silver prong settings

Using a setting is a very professional-looking way of incorporating stones that cannot be fired into metal clay pieces. You build the setting into the clay, fire, polish, and then gently bend the prongs over the stone to secure it.

Other jewelry-making supplies

You'll need a few other supplies to finish making your metal clay items into jewelry. Check the materials lists in the projects to see what's called for—items such as:
- **Jump rings** (outside diameter is listed in millimeters)
- **Earring wires**
- **Chain**
- **Clasps**

Molding compound

One of the handiest materials for molding is two-part silicone molding compound. Simply mix equal parts of each component together until the colors are blended, press in the item you want to mold, and set it aside for about five minutes to cure. You'll have a mold you can then use to make metal clay forms.

Basics

TOOLS & SUPPLIES

This section outlines the basic metal clay tool kit—the tools and supplies you'll need for making the projects in this book. I have tried to keep your start-up costs minimal by suggesting tools and, in some cases, substitutes, that are inexpensive, easy to come by, and low-tech. Some instructors or suppliers will sell kits similar to this to make it easy for you to get started.

Tools for working with wet clay

These are the basic "wet tools" that I use. Where you see a bulleted list, choose one among the alternatives; you don't need to have all of the options listed, especially as you're just getting started. As you progress, you may want to try adding a few tools or exploring options. Eventually you'll discover your favorites!

Underlay [A]
A smooth, easy-to-clean underlay is a must. This can be a glass cutting board or a smooth plastic sheet. Wipe it clean at the start of each work session to avoid transferring household debris such as dust or pet hair to the clay.

Plastic wrap [B]
Plastic wrap is my number-one must-have tool. Wrap clay scraps in it to keep them moist, store leftover clay in it, and use it to hold the clay as it is being conditioned. You can cut strips from a full-sized roll to make squares that are about 5".

Cutter/scraper [C]
Metal clay does not require anything super-sharp to get a nice cut. This cutter/scraper is a flexible piece of stainless steel. It is the tool I grab to lop off a bit of clay, or to trim long curved or straight edges.

Nonstick work surface
To make rolling and transporting the clay easy, always use some kind of nonstick sheet as a work surface. Keep several of these on hand, regardless of the type you choose. A 4–5" sheet is large enough; you will use a very small area at a time. I recommend rubbing a bit of olive oil or hand salve on the work surface to make the clay release easily. *Choose from:*
• **Freezer paper**
Freezer paper (not waxed paper or parchment paper) is a great option for a nonstick work surface. It is a disposable product that has no texture; clay rolled on it will be smooth on both sides and will release easily from the paper. It comes on a roll and can be found in the plastic wrap aisle of many supermarkets. Just cut it into 4" strips and cut each strip into five square pieces. Be sure to work on the plastic-coated side of the sheet. This paper can curl a bit, so place something heavy on the edges to keep clay from curling as it air-dries. Do not use freezer paper on a heated drying surface; the plastic coating can melt and the paper may burn.
• **Heavy plastic sheets**
Cut-up page protectors or other plastic sheets are another economical option. Use thick plastic; wrinkles will translate to the clay.

• **Flexible Teflon-coated sheets [D]**
Teflex sheets designed for baking are my favorite; they're very durable and don't curl up when heated. Both sides are suitable as a work surface, although wet clay rolled on these sheets will pick up a bit of pattern from the surface that you will have to sand off later. You can place these directly on a heated drying surface without worry; they won't melt.

Thickness gauges
Always use something to help you create a consistent thickness as you roll clay. *Choose from:*
• **Playing cards**
Playing cards are some of the most commonly used items for this purpose. In some instructions, you'll see direction to roll clay to "3 cards thick," for example. Playing cards that you stack and tape together in various thicknesses are a cheap solution to use as you're just getting started, but keep in mind that they are not the most reliable and consistent gauge.
• **Graduated slat sets [E]**
I love slats! These slats come in a set of paired, color-coded plastic strips that correspond to thicknesses of 1, 2, 3, 4, 6, and 8 cards. They also come with a millimeter conversion chart that lets you know the blue slats are 4 cards thick, which equals 1mm or .04" thick. I suggest you write

the thicknesses and conversions on each of the slats with a permanent marker. Be sure your roller stays on the slats at all times as you flatten the clay. Slats are easy to position on a rubber stamp as you roll a texture to a designated thickness.

A craft knife [F] is a good, multipurpose tool for everything from cutting paper templates to trimming the clay into fancy shapes to picking out bail holes. Some folks use disposable scalpels. Whichever you choose, use with care. They're sharp!

Self-healing cutting mat
These mats are handy when you use a craft knife to trim out paper templates. It will help keep your knife blade sharp longer, and will prevent you from accidentally cutting up your work surface.

Straws
Straws of all sizes are useful in many ways. **Cocktail or coffee stir straws [G]** are great for cutting small holes to hang pieces from. These and wider drinking straws can be used to make rolled bails. Fat straws for sipping boba tea (also known as "bubble" tea—that stuff made with tapioca pearls) are terrific forms for beads and slider pendants.

Roller [H]
A metal clay roller can be anything from a solid piece of acrylic to a piece of PVC pipe from the hardware store. A 6–8"-long cylinder with a 1" diameter is perfect. Grease it with olive oil or hand salve before you roll any clay. Avoid wood or aluminum rollers.

Salve and oil
All tools and work surfaces that contact wet clay need to be greased a bit to prevent sticking, and this includes your hands. You'll find several good options at the grocery store or drugstore. Do not use a petroleum-based product like Vaseline; it can degrade the binder in the clay. *Choose from:*

- **Hand salve [I]**
  A little goes a long way with these products. Burt's Bees and Badger Balm are two brands to try. I apply a bit to my hands, and then run my hands over the nonstick sheets and my roller to grease them. Hand salve is not a good release agent for rubber stamps; use olive oil for those.

- **Olive oil [J]**
  Olive oil is an easy-to-find and inexpensive lubricant. Go with a light olive oil for the longest shelf life. I have mine in a refillable spray bottle I got in the kitchen accessories department: Just pump and spray.

Needle tool
While not a "must-have," a fine-tipped needle tool can be used to trim wet clay. (As an alternative, you can use a long heavy-duty needle such as a darning needle.) This tool is especially useful with templates because it will cut through when pulled through the clay in any direction without damaging the template. Keep in mind that the needle tool will create a raised lip along the edge of the clay that must be sanded off later.

TOOLS & SUPPLIES

More wet-clay tools

Paintbrushes

A fine-tipped, pointed paintbrush with moderately stiff bristles will become your best metal clay friend. I use it for everything from spreading paste to moving syringe clay into place. I like a #0 or #1 sable brush. Get a high-quality brush and take good care of it for years of service. Never store the brush with its bristles down in a water cup as you work, or the bristles will be irreparably bent. A #4 (¼" wide) flat brush is helpful for quickly applying paste or slip to a large area. Also keep a **small cup of water** and a **roll of paper towels** within reach. Instructions sometimes call for using a moist paintbrush; this doesn't mean dripping wet! If you dip the brush into the cup and find you have too much, touch the tip of the brush on a paper towel to wick away some of the moisture.

Clay storage

Your clay must be stored in a humid environment so it does not dry out. Regardless of the method you choose, always keep the clay tightly wrapped in a piece of plastic wrap before it goes into its container. After long periods of time stored in plastic, the outside of the clay may turn yellow. This is nothing to worry about—the clay is fine. *Choose from:*

- **The pouch the clay comes in** is the most economical storage device. Place the wrapped clay in the pouch, add a piece of wet paper towel, and zip it up. The clay will stay moist for a couple of months. If you will not get back to the clay in that amount of time, moisten the paper towel and zip up the pouch again. You can keep the clay workable indefinitely like this.
- **Clay Keeper**
  This small plastic jar has a perforated plastic insert that keeps a wet sponge suspended above the wrapped clay. Check the sponge every few months and add water if needed. Even better, make your own from a baby food jar with a bit of wet sponge tightly closed inside.

Drying tools

Spatula [A]

The clay gets hot when you dry it with heat—it is metal, after all! Use a small spatula to move pieces on and off the drying surface. Give it a minute to cool before you touch it. (You don't want to pick it up, burn yourself, and then drop it on the floor, where it may shatter into pieces.) Look for a metal spatula with a wooden or insulated handle. Try a small (8" or so) offset icing spatula, a small cookie spatula, or even a mini spatula sold as a scrapbooking product.

Among drying equipment, you have choices ranging from tiny and cheap to high capacity and a bit more expensive. *Choose from:*

- **Candle warmer/mug warmer [B]**
  This is the drying method of choice at my workbench. It takes up very little space, provides a constant heat (around 200°F), and is easy to find and inexpensive (under $10). Pieces usually take about 20 minutes to dry on these warmers.

- **Oven or toaster oven**
  An oven, set at a low temperature of about 200°F is really convenient if you have many pieces to dry. You will also need a dedicated, nonaluminum baking sheet.

- **Other options**
  If you find you are making a lot of pieces, you can use a **food dehydrator** or an **electric griddle**. Look for a secondhand appliance and dedicate it to use with your clay.

Tools for working with dry clay

Micro files [A]
These tiny files, which are sold in a set of different shapes, are great for getting into small spaces. I use the round file the most because it fits into bails and straw holes, but the other shapes work well to refine irregular edges or cutouts in the clay.

Rubber block [B]
The rubber block is another indispensable item in your tool kit. Support your pieces on the block as you work from the dry state all the way through polishing. The block lifts your work up off the table so you can see it better, and it gives your hands much more room to maneuver around the piece. The slightly tacky surface helps keep your work in place.

Emery board [C]
Yes, I'm talking about the kind used for fingernails! Your local drugstore will have varieties and grits that you would never expect. Get a coarse one (about 150 grit) and a finer one (about 300 grit). These are used for straightening and smoothing straight edges.

Drill bits [D]
Keep a few drill bits in your kit for making small holes—just large enough for a jump ring to fit through. Try a #53 and higher; these will make 1.5mm and smaller holes. I keep my bit in a pin vise, which acts as a handle for the bit.

Dusting brush [E]
As you sand the clay, don't blow the dust into the air; you don't want to be breathing metal dust. Use a brush to gently remove the dust, gather it up, and use it to make more paste. An inexpensive eye-shadow brush is great for dusting metal clay away as you sand and file.

Sandpaper, sanding pads, and sanding swabs
Sanding is a controlled way to refine dry metal clay. There are many types of sanding supplies that are useful; I suggest you have at least these three on hand. If you want to reclaim your sanding dust, use a high-quality **sandpaper [F]**. Inexpensive ones will leave lots of gritty particles in the dust that causes black lumps in clay made with the dust. Keep several grits on hand: 180 and 320 grit are good for shaping; 600 and 1200 grit are good for removing sanding marks and polishing before firing. **Flexible sanding pads [G]** make sanding curved items easy and give a bit of cushion to the fingers. Look for the same grits as traditional sandpaper, 180–1200. **Sanding swabs [H]** are like gritty cotton swabs or sandpaper on a stick. I like to use the coarse ones to sand tight spaces and irregular or undulating shapes.

Mask
If you will be doing lots of sanding and filing or have respiratory issues, wear a N95 rated mask. You can pick one up at the hardware store. Your lungs will thank you.

TOOLS & SUPPLIES

Firing tools

Torch [A]

Butane torches are easy to operate and easy to refill. All butane torches are not created equal. My favorite is the Blazer SpitFire. When you are shopping for a torch, check the BTUs. In order for the silver to sinter properly, you need a torch with an output that is at least 2000–2500 BTU. (If there's no BTU listed, it is probably not hot enough.) Sometimes you can find a high-quality torch at a kitchen supply store, but I suggest going to a source that specializes in jewelry-making tools. Expect to pay around $60–$80 for a quality torch.

Some features to look for are:
- **Flame shape adjustment**
  This will allow you to customize the flame from a sharp flame (good for soldering) to a bushy flame that's best for sintering metal clay.
- **Gas output adjustment**
  This lever will let you release more or less fuel to adjust the size of the flame. This is especially handy if the cylinder is nearly empty—you can release more fuel to keep the flame size constant to finish a firing.
- **An auto-lock-on switch**
  Your fingers will thank you as this switch keeps the torch burning for 3–8 minutes, the amount of time you need to hold the clay in the flame.

Firebrick [B]

The dry clay piece must be placed on a special brick designed for firing (do not use a common building brick). Purchase a firebrick from the same source as your torch. They cost just a few dollars and are perfect for the job. The brick absorbs the heat and reflects it back up to the back of the piece. You do not need to flip items over to fire the other side.

Tweezers [C]

Keep a pair of tweezers nearby in case you need to move a hot piece.

Timer [D]

Such a simple yet important device! Look for a digital timer with buttons that are easy to push and a display that is easy to read in dim light. My favorite timer has an automatic reset to the last amount of time set. This will save you lots of button-pushing when firing several items one after the other. (It's also very useful for making many batches of cookies!)

Metal tray [E]

Using a metal tray will help keep your work surface free of brick dust. It also offers some protection in case your flame strays a bit, but remember that metal conducts heat, so the tray as well as the surface underneath can get hot.

Butane [F]

Butane fuel is fairly easy to find. Typically used to refill lighters, it is sold in small cylinders, often locked up near the cigarettes at the market. A 105-gram cylinder will fill a standard torch about a dozen times, and each of those fills is good for about four firings. Some higher-end torches (like the Blazer SpitFire) require triple-filtered butane, which burns cleaner and helps your torch last longer.

Quenching bowl [G]

A small stainless steel bowl filled with about 2" of water is perfect for flash-cooling (quenching) a hot, freshly fired piece.

Finishing tools

Sanding squares [A]

These are an inexpensive solution for creating a shiny finish on fired pieces. They come as a set of nine 2" foam squares in grits from 1,500-12,000. By working through the entire range, you can give your piece a gorgeous reflective surface.

Brass-bristle brush [B]

Get a high-quality brush with a long handle, soft bristles, and a wide head. I use this brush more than any other because it can be the first step toward a shiny finish or can create a final, satin finish. I always use my brush dry. Many recommend brushing with warm, soapy water. This is fine too, but you can't go back to using it dry after the brush has been exposed to water; it will turn your silver gray and dirty.

Steel-bristle brushes [C, D]

Short, sharp steel bristles in these brushes create visible stroke marks on the finished piece. The tiny version can fit almost anywhere, and can also be used to create scratched patterns in the silver because its bristles are extra stiff.

Burnisher [E]

Burnishers have smooth, rounded ends that are used to compress fine ridges of silver for a very shiny finish. They are usually either metal or agate (stone). A teaspoon is an economical substitute for a beginner.

Polishing cloth [F]

The last step in shining up a piece is to rub it with a soft polishing cloth that has jeweler's rouge built in. You can use one to remove naturally occurring tarnish or excess patina after a dip in liver of sulfur, a fast-acting oxidizer. A new cloth will turn black rather quickly; I use my old, nasty one to remove the bulk of blackness after a dip and a new one to finish up. Keep them in a zip-top bag to keep them at their best.

Pro polishing pads [G]

These are small squares of thin, dense micro-abrasive foam embedded with polishing compound. Use them dry; they're great in very tight spots.

Tools for adding patina

Liver of sulfur

Sulfur in the air will gradually oxidize silver over time. Some people call this tarnish and avoid it; others call it patina and love it. If you want to speed up the process, apply liver of sulfur (LOS) solution. You can enhance texture by polishing the raised surfaces and leaving the dark oxidation in the depressed areas. LOS is available in several forms. **Chunks [A]** must be dissolved in water; **gel [B]** is concentrated and results in a very colorful patina. LOS is also available as a liquid. You can apply the solution to specific areas with cotton swabs [C].

Glass bowls [D]

Custard dishes are especially nice because you can see the color of the solution (darker yellow is stronger). You'll need three: one for the LOS solution, one to rinse, and one for a neutralizing baking soda soak.

Tweezers [E]

Use nonreactive stainless steel tweezers to dip a piece into LOS solution. Get a long pair with small teeth at the tips to grip your work.

Nut pick [F]

An old-fashioned nut pick is handy for prying off the LOS can lid.

TOOLS & SUPPLIES

Specialty tools and supplies

The following are tools you'll need once in a while. It's a good idea to read through the project you plan to make and get familiar with any specialty tools I'm calling for beyond the basic kit.

Textures

Probably the number-one attribute of metal clay is that it can be textured easily with any number of things. Keep your eyes open; you may find a great texture in an unusual place. Texturing tools include:

- **Rubber stamps** are probably the most common tools for texturing metal clay. You'll usually place the stamp face up and roll clay over the top of it, so it's best to use stamp sheets that are large enough to support the slats as well as your clay.

- **Brass dies** have two key differences from rubber stamps. First, they create a crisp image because they are made from cut metal. Second, and more important, they create a raised rather than an impressed design. It is a beautiful, refined look.

- **Antique lace** works well as a texture because it's made of very crisp linen or cotton fibers. The threads make sharp cuts in the clay that look great after you add a patina. **Vinyl wallpaper** comes in an array of subtle textures. See if you can get sample swatches from your local home improvement store. Some online metal clay supply stores sell swatch sets for this purpose.

- You can make your own **molds** with silicone molding compound or buy them ready to go. Two-part molds let you make double-sided imprints.

- Tiny **metal stamps** cast or carved on the ends of steel rods are typically used for sheet metal, but they work great on metal clay as well. You can find fancy designs, as well as alphabets in lots of different fonts and sizes. Basic letter and number sets are available at discount tool supply stores. Also look for antique letterpress dies for unique flourishes. Leather-crafting alphabet and geometric stamps from your local craft store are also metal and are typically larger than the ones designed for use on sheet metal.

Forms

Many things around the house make great forms: spoons, marbles, light bulbs, even pillboxes can find their way into your tool kit to be used for shaping metal clay. Just be sure to avoid aluminum tools. Metal clay reacts with aluminum: It can get black spots, warp, deform, and, worst of all, break because the reaction prevents the silver from sintering properly. The wetter the clay is, the worse the results.

Cutters

Keep your eyes open for clay cutters—you'll find them everywhere. Most of my cutters are no larger than 1½" because my jewelry

pieces tend to be smaller than that. Your local craft store is a great place to start. Check out the polymer clay and cake-decorating aisles. You'll find some really cool fondant cutters that are superb for metal clay as well. Tiny brass cutters usually used for ceramics come in a huge array of sizes and basic geometric shapes. These are nice for tiny shapes because they have a plunger, which helps push out the clay if it gets stuck inside. Try cookie cutters too.

Clay shapers

Sometimes fingers are just too bulky to fit in the tight places you need to get into, and fingernails can get in the way, putting some ugly dings in the clay. Enter silicone-tipped clay shapers. The little wonders have wooden handles with flexible tips in an array of sizes, shapes, and stiffnesses. Use them to help you tuck in a bail, ruffle a leaf, blend a seam, and more. While these are not a necessity at first, they sure are helpful as you continue working with metal clay. I use a shaper with a soft, pointed tip most often and occasionally use a tapered, wedge-shaped tip. Cake fondant shapers are also useful for shaping metal clay.

Snake roller

Think back to childhood and how you would roll a piece of clay between your palms to make a long, thin snake. This tool works on the same principle, but you won't have to use your hands directly on the clay, causing it to dry out too quickly. A snake roller is a thick, clear rectangular piece of acrylic; it may or may not have a handle. (A scrap piece of acrylic will work just fine.) By moving it back and forth over a piece of moist clay, you'll end up with an even clay snake that can be used in many ways. You won't need it for every project, but I guarantee that you will need one of these often.

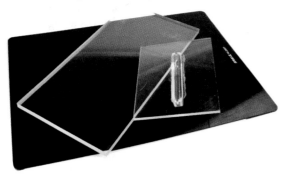

Ring sizer and mandrel

Traditional ring sizers consist of graduated sizes of bands held together on a big ring. Find the one that fits and read the size that is engraved on that ring. Ring sizers come in standard width and wide band styles; wide rings need to be larger to fit comfortably. Although a mandrel can be anything that you wrap something else around, if you plan to make a ring as in projects 13 and 14, you'll need a mandrel with precise ring sizes on it. It can be made of wood or metal. I suggest you get one on a stand that's easy to remove; it frees up both hands to work the clay.

Bead reamer and jewelry adhesive

If the hole in a half-drilled pearl is too small to accommodate a wire that you set in a clay piece, you can use a diamond-coated bead reamer to enlarge the hole: Insert it into the hole and twist. The tiny applicator of G-S Hypo Cement fits very nicely into the hole of a half-drilled pearl so you can easily and cleanly attach the pearl to a wire.

Prong pusher

Use a prong pusher to secure a stone in a prong setting. A very common style is made of a narrow piece of steel mounted in a wooden handle that fits in your palm. You'll also find pliers and tools designed for this purpose.

TOOLS & SUPPLIES

Fiber blanket

Fiber blanket is used to support irregularly shaped pieces during the firing process. Flat items are no problem because they are on a flat brick. Curved or wavy items need to have tiny bits of fiber blanket beneath them so every undulation is completely supported, otherwise, they will slump. Each bit of fiber reflects heat rather than absorbing it. Pieces of blanket can be reused, even though the texture will change (it gets rather crunchy). The blanket is made up of thousands of ceramic fibers pressed together. Just tear off the amount needed and tuck it under the dry piece. Wearing a mask while you're working with fiber blanket is a good idea; you don't want to get any bits in your eyes or breathe any of the free fibers. Wear gloves to handle it and be sure to wash your hands after touching it. Keep any unused blanket in a bag, away from kitchen items or eating surfaces.

Wet/dry sandpaper [A]

Use 600-, 1200-, and 2000-grit papers wet after a piece is fired to begin creating a shiny finish.

Polishing papers [B]

These micron-graded polishing papers (Tri-M-Ite by 3M is one brand) are soft and pliable, which makes them great for polishing just about any contoured surface. If I'm working toward a mirror finish, I use them after I sand with the finest grit of wet/dry sandpaper, starting with 1200 (blue) and moving through 4000 (pink), 6000 (mint), and 8000 (light green).

Tumbler and shot

Though not a necessity, a tumbler is very handy. This is the same equipment used by lapidaries. (Avoid children's rock tumblers from the craft store; they tend to be really loud and short-lived.) A tumbler serves several purposes: to give silver pieces a shiny finish effortlessly and to work-harden the surface of relatively soft fine silver. Rings especially benefit from some time in a tumbler. I especially like the small Lortone model 3A with its 3" barrel. Instead of using the sand and pellets that are used for rocks, use stainless steel shot (not regular steel, which will rust if not dried thoroughly between uses). I like to use a mix of shot shapes to get into all the nooks and crannies.

To tumble your silver clay pieces, first brush the fired silver with a brass brush. Put in 1–2 lbs. of shot, the silver pieces, water to cover by about ½", and ½ teaspoon of burnishing compound (or a few drops of blue Dawn dishwashing liquid). Plug in the tumbler and walk away for an hour. When you come back, rinse the contents of the barrel with fresh running water. You will be rewarded with sparkling silver creations!

Carving tools

Small carving tools such as those made by Dockyard and Speedball can be used to carve dry, unfired clay and to customize syringe tips.

Glazed tiles I use smooth 4x4" tiles from the hardware store to support delicate shapes as they dry.

Smooth-jaw tweezers

Small tweezers without ridges on the jaws will help you position shapes made from paper clay.

Tools and supplies for copper clay

If you want to try copper clay and make the pendant shown at the end of this book, you'll need a few more items and some dedicated tools. See p. 103 for more details.

TECHNIQUES

Metal clay has been available only since the 1990s. People are still discovering new and different ways of working. There are almost as many different ways of doing things as there are people using metal clay. The techniques presented here are those that work for my students and me. If you live in a really dry environment, you may want to set up a humidifier in the room as you work to help keep the clay pliable longer.

Working in the wet stage

Gram estimates

All of the projects in this book give you an amount of clay required in grams. Don't worry; you don't need a scale! All of these amounts are estimates anyway. If you're starting with a new 20-gram piece of clay, just lop off a fraction of the whole block using the guide on the right.

For scrap clay, ball up the clay and use these comparisons:

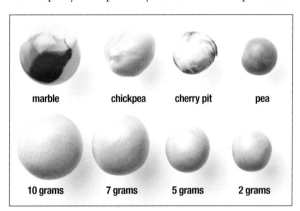

| marble | chickpea | cherry pit | pea |
| 10 grams | 7 grams | 5 grams | 2 grams |

Recovering scrap clay

"Clay begins to dry out the moment you open the package." Hearing those words from my first instructors always made me afraid to open the package for fear of wasting any little bit. My hands would shake, and I'd take a deep breath and hope for the best, knowing that I had to hurry—I was at the mercy of the clay, which was getting drier every second.

Then I learned about reconditioning leftover clay from the brilliant metal clay artist Gordon Uyehara, and all my anxiety fell away. With reconditioning, no clay is wasted; I learned I could make a mistake and still recover the clay. Totally liberating! My creativity flourished, and I hope knowing you can recover and reuse scrap clay will help you relax and enjoy working with the clay without worry (see p. 108 for the details).

Always keep any unused clay wrapped in plastic wrap. The longer clay is exposed to air, the more it will stiffen and crack and become unworkable. Tear off a strip of plastic wrap about 4" wide and use scissors to cut it in half.

I keep two pieces of plastic ready at all times: one for straight-out-of-the-package clay and one for my trimmings or goof-ups. Fresh clay that won't be used can go directly back into the plastic; after rolling or texturing and then collecting scraps, add a drop of water before placing the clay scraps into the plastic.

Storing clay between sessions

Clay must be kept in a moist environment or it will totally dry out between uses. Gather any unused clay and make sure it is moisturized well. Wrap it tightly in a piece of plastic wrap. Place it back in its packaging or other container with a wet sponge or bit of wet paper towel, and then tightly seal. Keep the container in a cool, dry place. Do not refrigerate or freeze.

Your clay should stay fresh for many weeks. If you still have not gotten back to the clay in that time, open the container back up, moisten, and reseal. You can keep clay going indefinitely like this.

TECHNIQUES

Wet stage (continued)

Setting up

Before you start a project, gather all the tools and materials that you will need for the wet stage of the project (slats, cutters, straws, roller, knife, plastic wrap, and paintbrushes). Think about what you are going to do before you open up the clay. Never roll out the clay and then try to pick out a rubber stamp or rummage around for a straw.

To set up your workspace, cover your tabletop with an underlay and place your nonstick sheet (Teflex or freezer paper) on top. Lightly grease anything that comes in contact with clay (this includes your hands). I apply a bit of salve or oil to my hands, and then run my hands over my roller and nonstick sheet. This thin coating is just enough to help release the clay. It should just look like a haze on the surfaces. If you can see finger marks or lots of shine, remove the excess with a paper towel.

Rolling clay

Before you roll out the clay, cut off the amount you need and give the clay a little squeeze. Don't knead it or fold it over itself. Place the clay on the nonstick sheet between the thickness gauge slats. Place the roller over the middle of the clay. Gently roll back and forth over the clay, working from the middle out.

Rolling this way gives you control over the shape of the clay. Pressing too hard initially creates an irregular shape that

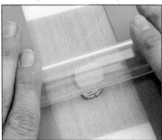

can't be changed. You can pick up the clay and move it around; just be sure to keep the roller on the slats. Roll until the clay shape doesn't grow, regardless of how hard you push.

Stamping

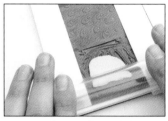

Hand salve is not a good release agent for rubber, so always use olive oil on rubber stamps. I keep my olive oil in a spritzer so I can apply a light mist to the stamp. Apply just a bit and them smear it around, getting it in all of the indentations in the stamp. If the stamp is extra-deep, use a dedicated brush to work the oil into the crevices. If you accidentally apply too much, use a paper towel to blot the excess.

Roll the clay one card/one slat thicker than the desired finished thickness. Flip the clay over onto the greased rubber stamp. Set slats that are the desired finished thickness on top of the stamp on either side of the clay. Place the roller on the slats in front of one end of the clay, roll with firm pressure all the way across the clay, and roll past the end of the clay. This will ensure an even impression. Don't roll more than once; multiple passes will cause double images that look very unprofessional.

Don't worry if the clay sticks to the roller a bit; just don't let it wrap entirely around and stick to itself. Gently peel the clay off the texture sheet. Flip it texture side up back onto the nonstick sheet. You'll get practice in rolling and texturing clay in the very first project.

Embossing

Embossing clay with a brass die creates a crisp, raised design. Roll the clay one card thicker than the desired finished thickness. Grease the die. Set the die on a piece of greased freezer paper. Roll to texture as you would with a rubber stamp. You'll work with a brass die in the "Hollow lentil beads" project.

Making holes using a straw

You can use a tiny straw to make a hole in a charm or pendant so you can attach a jump ring later. Make sure the straw is at least one straw's width away from the edge. Press the straw in, give a quarter-turn, and lift the straw out. Usually a plug of clay will be stuck in the straw. Pick it out and put it in your paste jar or mix it with your scrap clay. After the clay dries, smooth any rough spots by filing with a tiny round metal file.

Making holes with a drill bit

You can use a drill bit to make holes in wet clay, dry clay, or even fired clay with some elbow grease. Making small holes is always best done with a drill bit rather than poking with a pointy object. Drill bits remove some clay where the hole will go. Pointy objects just push the clay out of the way; they leave a puckery ring and uneven surface on the back of the piece. Holes made with drill bits will be smooth, flat, and pucker-free.

Balance the drill bit with your index finger while rotating the bit clockwise between your thumb and middle finger. Keep spinning it until the tip of the bit hits the work surface. For wet clay, set it aside to dry and then use the same drill bit from the reverse side to even out the hole.

Using syringe clay

Keep a small cup of water nearby to hold the syringe (tip down) as you pause during a work session. To use the syringe, hold it in the palm of your hand and depress the plunger with your thumb. Push out a bit of clay, tack it to the surface, and continue pushing the plunger as you lift the tip about ¼" off the surface. Let the clay fall into place. To end, stop pushing the plunger and gently touch the surface of the clay with the tip. If you're using syringe clay to seal a seam, you may get a little "ooze"—unruly extra clay. Just smooth the ooze with a moist paintbrush.

For long-term syringe storage, fold a 4x4" piece of plastic wrap into quarters. Unfold it and place a few drops of water in the middle of the square. Set the tip of the syringe in the puddle, wrap the plastic around the tip, and place the wrapped syringe in its foil pouch. Add a bit of wet paper towel and zip the pouch closed. Every month, if you have not worked with the syringe, remoisturize the paper towel and the inside of the plastic-wrap cone. By remoisturizing

like this, you won't waste any clay by having to clean out the tip. If you forget, usually replacing the syringe tip with a new one is all you need to do.

Working in the dry stage

This is my favorite stage of working with the clay because there is no time limitation and I can get as detailed as I want. The down side is that the clay is fragile. I call this the "potato chip" state: Pretend as though you are perfecting the finish on a delicate potato chip.

Sanding

This is the time to reshape wonky shapes, refine irregular edges, and smooth rough spots. Sanding is an easy, efficient way to take care of these things.

I recommend a 280-grit emery board for sanding straight or nearly straight edges. Place the piece on a rubber block.

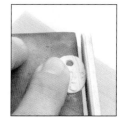

Hang just the edge of the piece over the edge of the block and hold it in place with your finger. If the piece is bowed, do not press down in the middle or you will break it! Position the emery board horizontally and move it back and forth along the edge until it is smooth. Rotate the piece and continue until all the edges are smooth. Do not sand up and down or you will break the piece on an upstroke.

For large, irregular edges, try using a small, folded piece of 280-grit sandpaper (another Gordon Uyehara trick I can't live without). Cut the sandpaper into 1½x½" pieces. Fold one in half and use it to get into all sorts of tight spots. This technique is especially useful for sanding rolled bails. Move a corner of the sandpaper in a circular motion up and over the bail.

Round shapes take a different approach. Set a strip of sandpaper on the rubber block. Roll the piece forward as you drag away from you across the sandpaper. Reposition your fingers and repeat all the way around. This method will prevent flat spots on round pieces.

Filing

Set the piece on a rubber block. Hang the edge of the piece off the side of the block. Use downward strokes of a mini or micro file to reshape the edges. Files are great

TECHNIQUES

Dry stage (continued)

because they come in many shapes to fit any contour. Files remove material only as you stroke in the direction the tip points, so do not use equal pressure and stroke back and forth; this will only increase the risk of breakage. Use a round file to tidy up the inside of any holes you made with a straw.

Drilling

If you forgot to make a hole in the wet clay, it is not too late. Balance the drill bit with your index finger while rotating the bit clockwise between your thumb and middle finger. With dry clay, you want to spin a lot and not push much at all. Let the bit shave away the clay. Keep spinning it until the tip of the bit hits the work surface. You should be ready to go with a nice perfect hole.

If you want to drill a hole 1mm or larger, make a pilot hole by drilling through with a smaller bit first. This will ensure the hole is positioned where you want it as well as reducing the risk of breakage.

Polishing before firing

Check the main surfaces of the clay for any imperfections: unwanted texture from the work mat, embedded hair, fingernail marks, tiny cracks, etc. If you see something, use very fine-grit sandpaper (2000 grit) to gently go over the surface of the clay until it is perfectly smooth. Just be careful—the clay sands so beautifully you can easily sand off your design. Imperfections can be removed after firing, but it takes a whole lot more elbow grease. Polishing before firing makes all of your finishing work much faster and easier.

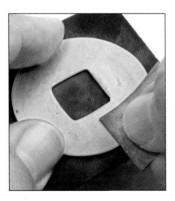

Torch-firing metal clay

Safety

Metal clay is nontoxic to work with—just don't eat it or let kids try to. Always use common sense. The binder that burns off produces carbon dioxide and steam. While considered harmless, it always makes sense to err on the side of caution. Fire in a well-ventilated area or outside. Wear cotton; avoid synthetic materials that can stick to the skin if burned. Also tie long hair back, wear closed-toed shoes, and don't wear loose-fitting clothes. Fire must always be respected—pay attention to what you are doing and avoid distractions.

Firing silver clay

Firing is the step that makes clay into metal ("sinters" the clay). The binder burns off and the silver particles are heated to a temperature that allows them to bond to each other, leaving 99.9% pure silver. As the silver particles heat and pull into each other, the clay shrinks. Different clays have different rates of shrinkage (see the Materials section for more details). The firing time and temperature determine the strength and rigidity of the finished product. Insufficient sintering produces a weak or brittle product.

As you begin to fire, I suggest that you dim the lights so you will be able to see the color of the clay most easily. Even better, invite a friend over so you have two more eyes on the piece. It is always helpful to have someone to consult about the color and worry about the timer for you!

 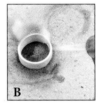 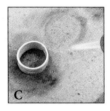

A　　　　B　　　　C

Working in a well-ventilated area (or outdoors), place the piece on a firebrick. (You may want to place the firebrick on a dedicated cookie sheet to contain any brick crumbles and help protect nearby areas from direct flame.) Light the torch. Working about 2" away, aim the flame at the piece and move it in a constant circular motion. (The distance can vary dramatically because of the intensity and shape of the flame, the amount of fuel in the torch, the type of fuel, and other factors). First you'll see a bit of smoke [A], and then the piece will catch fire for a few seconds [B]. Don't worry; just keep moving the torch in a circular motion. Next, the surface will turn white and the edges may begin to curl. Soon after that, you should be able to see a peachy glow coming from within

"I'm melting!"

Some things about firing: You can't fire too long (as long as you hold the correct temperature); the metal will just get stronger (to a point). However, you can overheat the piece; it can melt. Fortunately, there are warning signs along the way.

The first indication of overheating is the color of the piece changing from a nice peachy glow to what I like to call "hot lava." It will look bright orange, like it was just spewed from a volcano **[A]**. Just take the torch away just a bit and let the color return to peach.

If you ignore the "hot lava," next it will look like someone poured liquid mercury over the piece **[B]**. That is the surface of the silver liquefying. If you don't back off at that point, you'll end up with a ball of liquid silver dancing around the firebrick as the silver reaches its melting point of 1761°F.

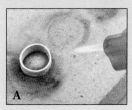 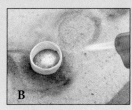

the piece, and any curled edges will begin to flatten [C]. That is when you start the timer. Firing duration is listed for each project in this book. It's based on the thickness of each piece and ranges from 3–8 minutes. Everything prior to this point does not count towards this time. If you need to stop for any reason, start over from the beginning of the firing instructions.

You can't torch-fire anything larger than a half-dollar (more than 25 grams of clay); the handheld torch doesn't generate enough heat.

The silver is incredibly hot after firing, over 1200°, so do not touch it! Let it cool naturally on the firebrick or wait a minute or so and then quench the piece. To quench, pick up the firebrick by holding the short ends. Tilt it away from you and let the silver piece slide into a bowl of water. After it sizzles, it is cool enough to grab out of the water. Dry it off and proceed to finishing.

Immediately after firing, the silver has a white surface. This is not a residue that must be removed, but rather the very irregular surface of the newly fired clay. Because the surface

is quite porous at this time, microscopically it is like a gravel road. This irregular surface reflects back all the colors of the light spectrum, which the human eye interprets as white. To see silver, you must smooth the surface so it becomes more reflective. The smoother it gets, the brighter and shinier the silver will look.

Finishing

Creating a scratch finish

You can brush your fired piece with a steel-bristle brush for a scratch finish. You will be making visible marks in the direction that you brush for a look like a stainless steel refrigerator. You can make marks that run vertically, horizontally, in a circle, or in a crosshatch pattern. Another way to create deliberate directional marks is to use very coarse sandpaper (100 grit).

Creating a satin finish

For a softer, slightly shinier look, use a brass-bristle brush for a satin finish. No brush marks will be visible, so you can brush in any direction. Satin is a lovely finish for many styles of work.

Creating a shiny finish

For a shiny finish, begin with the brass-bristle brush. Next, use the sanding squares—all of them! Start with the coarsest one. Really put your time and effort behind this one; it does so much of the work of removing any imperfections in the surface. Don't quit until everything unwanted is gone, because all of the subsequent grits of sanding squares remove only the scratch marks of the previous square.

Take your time and work carefully if you want a super-shiny finish. By the time you get to the last square, you should be able to see your reflection in the silver. The more elbow grease you expend, the better the result will be! There are many different ways of polishing your silver pieces. This is a straightforward technique that is low cost.

Another inexpensive option is using wet/dry sandpaper. Working at a sink under a trickle of water, place the piece on a rubber block. Sand the surface with 600-grit paper until all the surface imperfections are gone. Move to 1200 grit and

Finishing (continued)

then 2000 grit. Switch to fine-grit Tri-M-Ite papers and work through all the grits in order.

There are countless terrific mechanical options for polishing that are more expensive and require investment in special equipment. Although I won't detail those here, be aware that if you have hand-strength issues or like to keep your nails beautifully manicured, you can find lots of other ways to get the job done.

Burnishing

Burnishing is a method of compacting the surface of the silver firmly with a tool. Burnishing tools made specifically for use on metal will produce a very shiny result, but it's not for all pieces. If you use this tool at all, please use it to shine only very fine lines or very narrow areas of clay such as the veins of these silver leaves. If used on a larger area, the curved tool will leave visible indentations in the clay.

Adding patina

After the piece is polished to your desired finish, think about whether a patina that darkens or colors the surface would enhance the texture. Liver of sulfur (LOS) is a versatile patina product because it can create various colors as well as dark gray. When a fired silver clay piece is dipped into the solution, first it will turn golden, and then it will progress through greens, pinks, blues, and eventually dark gray. The rate at which it moves through these colors has to do with the amount of LOS in the water (more=faster), the temperature of the water (hotter=faster), and the duration of immersion (longer=darker).

The effect that the solution will have varies depending on what type of finish the silver clay piece has. Because the surface is still really porous, items with a scratch finish will end up darker, kind of like pewter, with little contrast between the main surface and the depressed design [A]. You'll get more contrast on silver with a satin finish [B]. Silver with a shiny finish will show

A

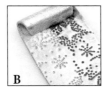

B

the most contrast because the surface is very smooth and the polishing cloth will remove almost all of the patina from the raised surfaces, leaving the dark colors in the relief surfaces [C]. Pieces with a shiny finish also tend to develop bright pinks and blues best.

C

To prepare for using an LOS solution, set out three small bowls (clear glass works well). Fill one with cold water. Fill another with a tablespoon or two of baking soda mixed with ½ cup cold water and set aside. To mix the solution, dissolve a pea-sized chunk or ¼ tsp. of gel in a third bowl filled with 6 oz. of hot water (not quite boiling). Stir with tweezers until the chunk is dissolved or the gel is dispersed. The solution should be about the color of apple juice. Dunk the piece into the solution using tweezers. Hold onto the piece in case you get a terrific color that you want to keep; you'll need to pull it out right away and rinse it in the bowl of plain water to stop the reaction. You can redip and

rinse as many times as desired. When you are satisfied with the color(s), rinse and then soak the piece in the prepared neutralizing baking soda solution for a few minutes. This will help prevent the silver from continuing to react. Rinse again under fresh water and dry the piece. If you got amazing colors that you want to keep, use the polishing cloth sparingly to reveal highlights of silver. The "Mosaic pendant" project gives you more tips on getting color out of LOS.

If you want to darken the piece more but have already used a polishing cloth, wet the piece, sprinkle with baking soda, and rub. Rinse and dry. This will remove any polishing residue that might prevent the liver of sulfur from reacting. Redip and continue as before.

If you are totally unhappy with the results, you can place the piece back on the firebrick and heat it with a torch until the patina burns off. You may need to touch up the polishing a bit.

Silver will gradually darken over time as it's exposed to the air, so plan on touching up with the polishing cloth as needed. Because fine silver has no copper in its makeup (as sterling silver does), it is slow to tarnish. Neutralize LOS before disposal by letting it sit until it turns cloudy white.

BASIC METAL CLAY TOOL KIT

(needed for every project)

Tools for working with wet clay

- ☐ Underlay
- ☐ Nonstick work surface (choose from):
  - • Freezer paper
  - • Heavy plastic sheets
  - • Flexible Teflon-coated sheets
- ☐ Roller
- ☐ Thickness gauges (choose from):
  - • Playing cards
  - • Graduated slat set
- ☐ Cutting tools
  - • Cutter/scraper
  - • Craft knife
  - • Self-healing cutting mat
  - • Needle tool
- ☐ Straws of various sizes
- ☐ Drill bits—1mm and 1.5mm
- ☐ Paintbrushes—#1 and #4
- ☐ Plastic wrap
- ☐ Lubricants (choose from):
  - • Hand salve
  - • Olive oil
- ☐ Cup of water
- ☐ Paper towels
- ☐ Clay storage (choose from):
  - • Pouch the clay comes in
  - • Clay Keeper

Drying tools

- ☐ Choose from:
  - • Candle/mug warmer with spatula
  - • Oven or toaster oven
  - • Food dehydrator
  - • Electric griddle with spatula

Tools for working with dry clay

- ☐ Rubber block
- ☐ Sanding supplies
  - • Sandpaper
  - • Sanding pads
  - • Emery boards
  - • Sanding swabs (optional)
- ☐ Dusting brush
- ☐ Drill bit in pin vise
- ☐ Micro files
- ☐ Dust mask (optional)

Firing tools

- ☐ Torch
- ☐ Butane fuel
- ☐ Firebrick
- ☐ Metal tray
- ☐ Tweezers
- ☐ Timer
- ☐ Quenching bowl

Finishing tools

- ☐ Steel-bristle brush
- ☐ Brass-bristle brush
- ☐ Set of sanding squares—1,500 to 12,000 grit
- ☐ Burnisher
- ☐ Polishing cloth
- ☐ Pro polishing pads (optional)

UTILITY TOOLS & SUPPLIES

(always have on hand)

- ☐ Ruler
- ☐ Scissors
- ☐ Pencil
- ☐ Clear tape
- ☐ Paper towels
- ☐ Small cup of water

SPECIALTY TOOLS & SUPPLIES

(needed occasionally—check list at beginning of project)

Patina setup

- ☐ Glass bowls
- ☐ Liver of sulfur
- ☐ Nut pick (optional)
- ☐ Tweezers
- ☐ Cotton swabs
- ☐ Baking soda

Other specialty tools & supplies

- ☐ Textures
  - • Rubber stamps
  - • Brass dies
  - • Lace and wallpaper
  - • Molds
  - • Metal stamps
- ☐ Forms—spoons, marble, etc.
- ☐ Cutters
- ☐ Shaping tools
- ☐ Snake roller
- ☐ Ring sizer and mandrel
- ☐ Bead reamer and jewelry adhesive
- ☐ Prong pusher
- ☐ Fiber blanket
- ☐ Polishing papers
- ☐ Wet/dry sandpaper—600, 1200, and 2000 grit
- ☐ Tri-M-Ite polishing papers
- ☐ Tumbler and shot (optional)
- ☐ Jewelry-making tools
  - • Flush cutters
  - • Chainnose pliers
  - • Flatnose pliers
  - • Roundnose pliers

Are you excited to begin making metal clay jewelry? Great! You'll find the easiest projects in the beginning of the next section. The projects are grouped by the techniques you'll learn, starting with basic techniques and moving through stone-setting, syringe clay, forming, and special techniques. It's terrific if you work through the projects in order. You'll build your skills with each project you complete. If you decide not to make all of the projects, at least read through them—you won't want to miss helpful tips as I explain techniques in detail at the start. As we move on, I assume that you've got the basics under your belt, and the projects start to get a little more challenging.

Let's get started!

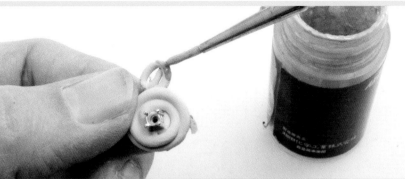

Projects

PROJECT1
Stamped charms

Get started with the basics and learn how to be in control of the clay! Practice rolling the clay and getting the shape you want. Learn how to get a clean impression with a rubber stamp. End with neat holes for a professional finish.

Finished height: ¾" (largest charm)

WHAT YOU'LL NEED

Basics
- 10 grams Art Clay Silver 650 or PMC+
- Metal clay tool kit
- Patina setup (optional)

Specialty tools
- Rubber stamps
- ½–1" small clay cutters, various shapes

How to begin any project

Set up your workspace, placing a nonstick sheet on your underlay. Rub a very light coating of olive oil or hand salve on anything that comes in contact with the clay, including your hands. Read ahead in the directions so you know the steps to come: First you'll cut off the amount of clay you need and give it a little squeeze; don't knead it or fold it over itself. Place the clay on the nonstick sheet between the slats. Set the roller down in the middle of the clay. Gently roll back and forth over the clay, working from the middle out. This will give you a lot of control over the shape of the clay. Aim for rolling a fairly uniform oval or circle of clay. Pressing too hard initially will cause an irregular shape that can't be changed. Feel free to pick up the clay and move it around; just be sure the roller stays on the slats at all times.

TIP

If you're using Teflex as your nonstick sheet, the clay may pick up some unwanted texture from its woven surface. Just flip the clay over so the side that was touching the roller is the side that touches the stamp.

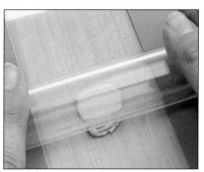

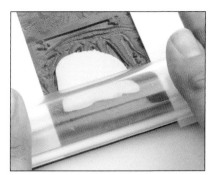

Roll and shape the clay

1. Working quickly, cut and then roll about a third of the clay (3 grams or so). Use slats or playing card stacks to roll the clay to 3 cards thick. Wrap any unused clay tightly in a piece of plastic wrap.

2. Flip the clay over onto the greased rubber stamp. Set 2-card-thick slats or card stacks on either side of the clay, making sure they are on top of the stamp. Texture the clay by making one firm pass over the clay.

3. Gently peel the clay off the texture sheet and place it texture side up on the nonstick sheet. Holding the sides of the cutter, press it firmly into the clay to trim out the shape. (If your cutter has a plunger, don't press it while cutting the clay; lift the cutter and then, if the clay is stuck, gently press the plunger to push the charm out.) Preserve any scrap clay.

TIP When texturing clay, always pass the roller over the clay only once. Multiple rolls will cause double images that look very unprofessional. Place the roller before the clay. Start rolling with firm pressure all the way across the clay and keep going past the end of the clay. This will ensure that the impression is nice and even all the way across the surface. Don't worry if the clay sticks to the roller a bit. (But pause and peel the clay off if it begins to wrap all the way around the roller—you don't want it sticking to itself!)

4. Place a stir straw at least one straw width away from the edge. Press the straw in, rotate it a quarter-turn, and lift the straw out. A plug of clay will usually remain in the straw; pick it out and put it in your paste jar or mix it in with your scrap clay.

5. Using the remaining clay, follow steps 1–4 to make several more charms. Now that you have some experience, you can make several at the same time.

Dry and refine the charms

6. Set the wet pieces on the mug warmer to dry. Be careful—they get very hot!

7. In the dry state, clay is very fragile. Be careful handling the charms; think of them as potato chips! After the charms are completely dry, smooth one charm at a time, supporting the piece on a rubber block as you work. Hang the edge of the charm over the edge. Use sandpaper or an emery board with a grit anywhere from 150 to 300 to refine the edges and finalize the shape.

TIP A piece that is not quite dry enough to fire may feel a bit clammy. Another test is to set it on a mirror for 30 seconds. When you lift it up, if you see fog on the mirror, dry it more.

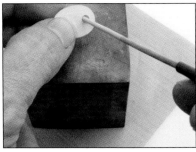

8. Take as much time as you like for this stage. Use a very fine-grit sandpaper, about 2000 grit, to gently smooth any imperfections in the textured surface. Use a light touch; you can easily sand off the design. Smooth the back of each charm with fine-grit sandpaper as well.

TIP

Sand over a piece of paper so you can easily collect the dust. When you are finished, transfer the dust to your paste jar and add a few drops of water. You just made more paste!

9. Use a small round file to smooth the inside of the straw hole.

Fire

10. Be sure the piece is completely dry before firing; steam generated by moisture in the clay might cause the piece to rupture. Set a few charms on the firebrick as close together as possible, almost touching. Make sure the area covered is no larger than a half-dollar. Fire for 3 minutes (refer to the Basics section for more details). Pick up the brick from the sides and slide the pieces into a bowl of cold water to quench. As soon as they sizzle, they are cool enough to touch. Dry.

ANOTHER IDEA

If you roll about 7 grams of clay and texture it exactly as described for the charms, you will have plenty of clay left from a standard package to make a pendant for a V-shaped necklace. Make a hole on the top left and top right and connect each side to a chain with jump rings.

Finish and polish
11. After firing, the silver will have a matte white surface. Brush each charm with a brass-bristle brush for a satin finish.

12. You have the option at this point to use a liver of sulfur solution that will enhance the texture with an antique look (see p. 26 for full instructions). When the charm is a color you like, transfer it to cold water, dry, and use the polishing cloth to reveal a brilliant shine.

PROJECT2
Mobile earrings

These kinetic earrings show off the beauty of scratch-finished silver. They are quick to make because the inside of one shape is the outside of the next!

TIP Freezer paper (not wax paper or parchment paper) is a great alternative to Teflex sheets for rolling out clay. The plastic-coated surface is super-smooth and, when greased a bit, releases the clay beautifully. I use freezer paper whenever I want to be sure there is no visible texture from the Teflex after rolling out the clay. This is especially important in situations where the shape of the piece makes it hard to sand the texture off later.

Finished length: 2"

WHAT YOU'LL NEED

Basics
- 20 grams Art Clay Silver 650 or PMC+
- Freezer paper
- 16 3mm jump rings, 22 gauge
- Pair of earring wires
- Metal clay tool kit

Specialty tools
- Concentric clay cutters: ¼", ½", and ¾" ovals
- 1mm and 1.5mm drill bits (#60 and #53)
- 2 pairs of flatnose pliers
- Bead reamer (optional)

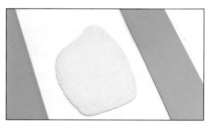

Roll and shape the clay

1. Set up your workspace, using a rectangle of freezer paper for your nonstick sheet. Rub a very light coating of olive oil or hand salve on anything that will touch the clay, including the freezer paper. Cut 10 grams of the clay and wrap the unused clay tightly in a piece of plastic wrap. Working quickly, roll the clay to 3 cards thick on the freezer paper.

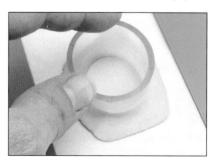

2. Cut out largest oval.

3. Remove the outer extra clay and preserve. Cut out the center of the oval using the medium cutter.

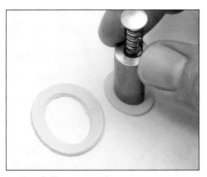

4. Carefully remove the center negative space, place it to the right of the first oval, and cut out the center of the second oval using the small cutter. Carefully separate each shape so you have two rings and a center oval.

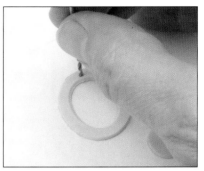

5. While the clay is still wet, use a #53 drill bit to make a 1.5mm hole in the top and bottom of the large ring. To make a hole with a drill bit, balance the bit with your index finger while rotating it clockwise with your thumb and middle finger. Use a #60 drill bit to make a 1mm hole in the tops of the remaining shapes. Dry the clay.

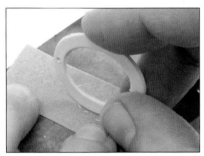

6. Place sandpaper on top of the rubber block. Carefully sand the outer edges of the large ring by rolling it over the sandpaper.

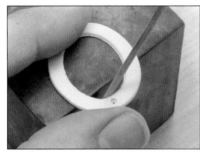

7. Use a small half-round file to smooth the inside edges. Smooth the other pieces in a similar way.

8. Use the drill bit to open the holes, working from the back. Sand all surfaces smooth.

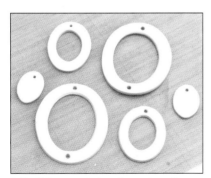

9. Roll the remaining clay to 3 cards thick and repeat steps 2–8 to make three more shapes in the same way.

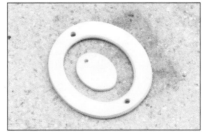

Fire

10. Place the smallest piece inside the largest on the firebrick. Fire for 3 minutes. Pick up the brick from the sides and slide the pieces into a bowl of cold water to quench. As soon as they sizzle, they are cool enough to touch. Dry. Repeat for second set of large ring and small oval.

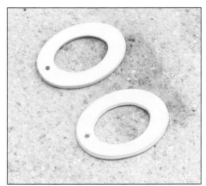

11. Place the two medium rings together on the brick as close together as possible. Fire for 3 minutes. Quench. Dry.

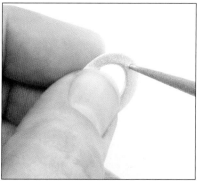

Finish and polish

12. Brush each charm with a steel-bristle brush for a scratch finish. This brush will leave marks, so work in a deliberate pattern. Work your way around the surface until you like the texture and the white finish has turned silver.

13. Check the fit of the jump rings in the holes. If they do not fit, use a diamond-tipped reamer to enlarge the holes a bit by twisting the reamer several times in the hole.

14. Assemble the earrings by hanging each small oval inside a large ring with a chain of three jump rings. Hang each medium ring from a large ring with a chain of three jump rings. Attach the earring wires to the top of the large rings with two jump rings, sharing the hole at the top.

Use drill bits to make clean holes

Making small holes is always best done with a drill bit vs. a pointy object. Drill bits will actually remove the clay where the hole will go. Pointy objects just push the clay out of the way. From the front, they don't look much different, but from the back there is a huge difference. The back of the pointy-object hole will have a puckery ring around the piercing and the clay will not be flat anymore. Holes made with drill bits will be smooth, even, flat, and pucker-free. Use a drill bit to make a hole in the clay for attaching a jump ring later.

ANOTHER IDEA

If you have four concentric shape cutters, you can make a pendant with shapes that nest inside each other! This does take some gentle sanding, as you have to remove a bit of clay from the inside and outside of each shape to make room for all the jump rings. These would also be great as a bold pair of earrings.

How to open and close jump rings

Use two pairs of chainnose pliers (or one chainnose and one flatnose) to grip the ends of the ring. Push one pair away and move one toward you to open the ring. Add a closed ring or other component with a loop, and close the jump ring by moving the pliers in the opposite way.

PROJECT3

Antique coin pendant

Create a dramatic focal piece reminiscent of old Chinese currency. You'll place a barrier on the stamp to create a smooth, recessed area that contrasts well with the textured surface. This pendant looks especially nice if you give it a shiny finish.

Finished diameter: 1⅜"

WHAT YOU'LL NEED

Basics
- 15 grams Art Clay Silver 650 or PMC+
- Card stock scrap
- Silk ribbon (3')
- Metal clay tool kit
- Patina setup

Specialty tools
- Rubber stamp with shallow, random design
- ½" square clay cutter
- 1¼" circle clay cutter or template
- 1½" circle clay cutter
- Small metal stamps (optional)

TIP

For this project, you can use a circle template or a compass to create the 1¼" circle in step 1.

For the stamp in step 2, I recommend using a random design that's not very deep.

Make a template

1. Using the 1¼" cutter as a guide, trace around the outside onto the card stock.

2. Carefully trim out the circle and grease this paper template. Lay the template on the stamp, greased side up, and set aside.

Roll and shape the clay

3. Set up your workspace. Rub a very light coating of olive oil or hand salve on anything that will touch the clay, including the rubber stamp. Roll 15 grams of clay to 4 cards thick.

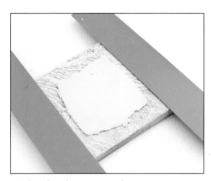

4. Flip the clay over and center it over the template on the stamp. Place 3-card-thick slats or card stacks on the stamp alongside the clay. Texture the clay by passing the roller over the clay once firmly.

5. Gently peel the clay off the stamp and peel off the template. Set the clay back on the nonstick sheet. You should have a textured area with a perfectly smooth circle in the middle.

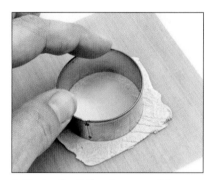

6. Center the 1½" cutter around the smooth circle and cut.

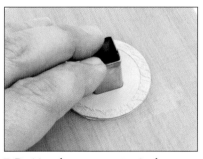

7. Position the square cutter in the middle of the circle. Cut.

8. Remove the excess clay with the tip of a craft knife.

9. If desired, use small metal stamps to add design elements around the square cutout. Dry the clay.

TIP Are you remembering to preserve all your clay scraps? Notice that I'm not reminding you anymore!

Refine

10. Place a small piece of 180-grit sandpaper on the rubber block. Smooth the edges and avoid flat spots by rolling the piece on the sandpaper.

11. Fold the sandpaper in half and use it to shape a slightly rounded edge on the front and back of the piece.

12. Smooth the front and back of the square opening.

13. Notice how the back of the piece has a faint texture from the nonstick sheet. Working on the rubber block, smooth the entire back with a progression of folded 600-, 1200-, and 2000-grit sandpaper using a gentle circular motion. If the piece is bowed, use very gentle pressure so it doesn't crack.

Fire

14. Place the pendant on a firebrick and fire for 3 minutes. Pick up the brick from the sides and slide the pendant into a bowl of water to quench.

ANOTHER IDEA

Use a small paper heart as

a mask to create a smooth area inside a larger textured heart, and then customize the smooth area with letter stamps. The untextured area really helps the lettering stand out. This pendant reminds me of the proclamations of love young people carve in trees.

Finish and polish
15. Brush the front with a brass-bristle brush.

16. On the back, use a small, steel-bristle brush to create a scratch finish of strokes radiating out from the center. Flip over.

TIP

Use a permanent marker to code your sanding squares with numbers representing the order of use.

TIP

It can be hard to know when to switch from one grit to the next. As you finish with the coarsest square, make a final pass over the entire surface vertically. Turn the piece 90 degrees and use the next-finer grit vertically. As soon as all the horizontal scratch marks are gone, it is time to switch to the next finer grit. Turn the piece 90 degrees and repeat until you have gone through the entire stack of sanding squares.

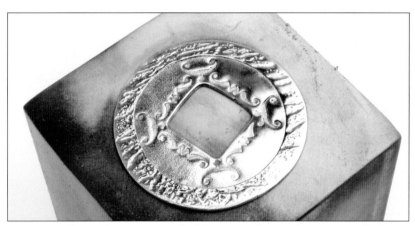

17. Next use the sanding squares—all of them! Spend most of your time and effort with the coarsest one: It does all of the work removing any surface imperfections. Notice the difference between the right and left sides; the right side has been sanded until all the surface imperfections are gone, and all you see are the scratch marks from the sandpaper. The subsequent grits will remove the scratch marks of the previous sanding square. Take your time and work hard if you want a super-shiny finish. By the time you get to the last square, you should see your reflection.

18. Dip the piece in a liver of sulfur solution until it is darkened. Rinse, neutralize, and dry. Use a polishing pad or cloth to restore the highlights.

19. Fold the silk ribbon in half and pull a few inches of the fold through the hole of the pendant.

20. Pull the free ends of the ribbon through the loop and pull tight. You've just made a lark's head knot—an easy way to turn a donut pendant into a necklace.

PROJECT4
Ginkgo pendant

The ginkgo is an ancient eastern symbol of strength and longevity, and its leaves are a common theme for jewelry items. This delicate pendant features a challenging narrow rolled bail. This project will help you get comfortable cutting irregular shapes with a craft knife. It is quick to polish with a satisfying contrast of satin finish and shiny, burnished ridges.

Finished width: 1¾"

WHAT YOU'LL NEED

Basics
- 10 grams Art Clay Silver 650 or PMC+
- Art Clay Silver 650 Paste or PMC+ Slip (optional)
- Art Clay Silver 650 Syringe, green tip or PMC+ Syringe, pink tip
- Metal clay tool kit

Specialty tools
- Ginkgo rubber stamp sheet
- Pointed-tip clay shaper
- Burnishing tool
- Sanding swabs (optional)

Roll and shape the clay

1. Set up your workspace. Rub a very light coating of olive oil or hand salve on anything that will touch the clay, including the rubber stamp. Working quickly, roll the clay to 4 cards thick.

2. Check the stamp size and shape as you roll to be sure you have enough clay to cover the design. Allow about ½" of extra clay at the top for the bail (the rolled extension at the top that allows the pendant to be strung on a chain or cord).

3. Texture the clay at 3 cards thick by making one firm roll over the clay.

4. Place the clay textured side up on a nonstick sheet. Quickly trim the stem half of the leaf shape with a craft knife, making the stem at least 4mm wide.

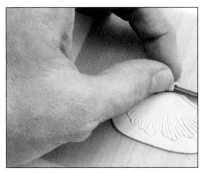

5. Trim the stem end straight. We'll roll the bail quickly to prevent cracking, and finish trimming in a later step. Working near one end of the stir straw, roll the stem end forward around the straw until it touches the face of the pendant.

6. Roll the clay back a bit and apply a bead of syringe along the cut edge of the clay. Roll the clay forward and hold it in place for a moment.

7. Use a clay shaper to tuck the clay into a neat tube.

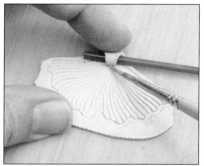

8. Use a moist brush to smooth any "ooze," or stray syringe clay, up onto the rolled bail. (It will be much easier to sand any remains off the smooth bail rather than off the textured pendant.)

9. Trim the remaining part of the pendant. Leave the straw in place and set the piece aside to dry.

Refine

10. When the pendant is completely dry, gently twist the straw and pull it out while supporting the bail.

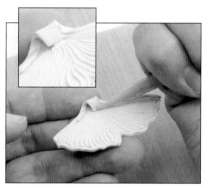

11. Check if the bail is fully attached. If you see any gaps, apply another bead of syringe "caulk" along the seam and smooth with a damp brush.

The rolled bail is an easy-to-make finish for just about any pendant. Make a narrow bail to give the overall piece the look of a shield, as in this Celtic crest design. (This pendant was one of the first projects that my husband made in metal clay.)

TIP

Always use more paste than you think you need because the level of the silver will go down as the water evaporates.

12. If you see any cracks in the bail, moisten them and use a paintbrush to fill them with a generous layer of paste. Dry again. Repeat until all cracks and seams are filled.

13. Supporting the piece on a rubber block, use sandpaper to refine edges, finalize the shape, and smooth any repairs. Take as much time as you want, being careful not to sand away the stamped design as you refine the shape.

Fire

15. Place the piece on the firebrick. Fire for about 3 minutes. Drop into a bowl of cold water to quench. Dry.

Finish and polish

16. Brush the piece with a brass brush.

14. On the bail, smooth the areas where you applied paste with the corner of a folded piece of 200-grit sandpaper. Move smoothly up and over the bail.

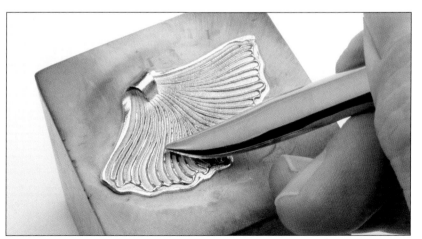

TIP

Do not use the burnishing tool as an overall polishing technique! The burnishing tool is best used on very thin, detailed areas; it will leave coarse marks on broad surfaces.

17. Rub the burnishing tool firmly along the length of each thin, raised vein. This will compress and shine the silver to provide a nice contrast with the satin finish of the background. To polish the inside of the bail, insert the coarsest sanding swab and twirl. Repeat with finer-grit swabs.

PROJECT5
Draped lace pendant

With its crisp details, fine lace is terrific to use for texturing clay. Emboss textures on both sides of this pendant and then drape the clay over dowels to create this rippling, reversible pendant. You'll also learn how to support the clay during firing so it keeps its flowing shape.

Finished length: 2"

WHAT YOU'LL NEED

Basics
- 10 grams Art Clay Silver 650 or PMC+
- Art Clay Silver 650 syringe, green tip, or PMC+ syringe, pink tip
- Freezer paper
- Metal clay tool kit

Specialty tools & supplies
- 2 textures of fine lace trim or netting
- Small spray bottle with water (optional)
- 3 wood dowels (⅛–¼" diameter)
- Toothpicks
- Pointed-tip clay shaper
- Pin vise with 1mm drill bit (#60) (optional)
- Fiber blanket

Prepare the dowels
1. Sand one end of each dowel so it's tapered and smooth. This will ensure that the dowels won't mar the clay.

Roll and texture the clay
2. Set up your workspace, using a rectangle of greased freezer paper for your nonstick sheet. Rub a very light coating of olive oil or hand salve on any other tools and supplies that will touch the clay except the lace.

3. Working quickly, roll all 10 grams of clay to 4 cards thick, shaping it into a long rectangle. Place one lace texture on the freezer paper and cover it with the clay. Place a second lace texture over the clay.

4. Place 4-card slats or card stacks on both sides of the clay, making sure the textures are not on top of them. Roll again.

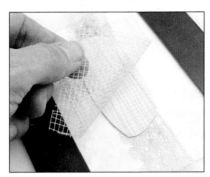

5. Carefully peel the top texture away. Lift the clay, peel off the second texture, and place the clay back on the freezer paper.

6. Trim the sides straight with the cutter/scraper or a craft knife. I left a natural curve at the bottom edge.

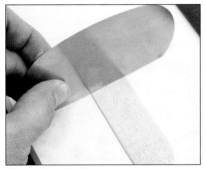

Make the bail

7. Trim the top edge straight. Decide which texture is the front, and, if necessary, flip the clay over so the front faces down.

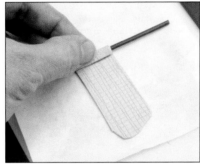

8. Roll the top edge of the clay forward around a greased stir straw until it touches the front of the pendant.

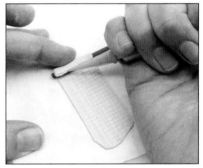

9. Unroll the clay just a bit so you can apply a line of syringe clay along the cut edge. Roll the clay so it touches the pendant front again and hold it in place for a moment.

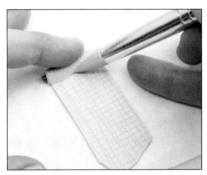

10. Use a clay shaper to help you tuck the clay in, making a neat tube. Use a moist brush to smooth any ooze up and onto the bail.

Shape and drape the clay

11. Gently drape the clay over greased wooden dowels to create several smooth curves. Use the clay shaper to help ease the clay down around the dowels. If the clay begins to dry out, lightly mist it with water, cover lightly with plastic wrap, and let it sit for a few minutes. Continue shaping the clay.

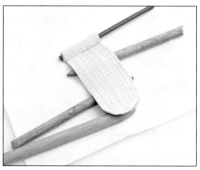

12. Set the shape aside to dry completely with the dowels in place.

Refine the shape

13. Gently remove the straw. Use sandpaper to refine the edges and finalize the shape.

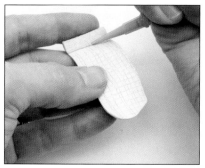

14. Add more syringe clay as necessary to smooth and secure the seam of the rolled bail.

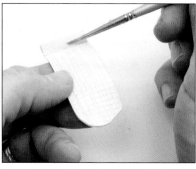

15. Use a moist brush to smooth the seam carefully so you don't obscure the design.

Fire

16. Support each ripple with a bit of fiber blanket on the firebrick. Fire for 3 minutes. Cool naturally.

Finish

17. Brush with a brass-bristle brush.

CAUTION Wear a mask when using fiber blanket and wash your hands afterward. You do not want to breathe loose fibers or get them in your eyes.

ANOTHER IDEA

Give the lace extra dimension by adding holes that
follow the pattern of the lace. I used a handheld rotary tool and a fine drill bit to drill lots of holes quickly and easily after the clay was dry but before I fired it. You can also drill without power using just a drill bit (or a bit held in a pin vise). Either way, take your time and work carefully. Another idea is to create a more fluid shape and use a liver of sulfur solution to enhance the texture of the lace.

PROJECT 6
Bejeweled cobra earrings

Here's a great use for those little leftover pieces of clay. It takes just a few grams to make each of these earrings. They are fun to make and give you lots of practice with properly conditioning the clay as well as rolling and manipulating snakes. To add sparkle, you'll secure colorful cubic zirconias in prong settings.

Finished length: ¾"

WHAT YOU'LL NEED

Basics
- 7 grams Art Clay Silver 650 or PMC+
- Art Clay Silver 650 Paste or PMC+ Slip
- Art Clay Silver 650 Syringe, green tip, or PMC+, pink tip
- 2 3mm fine silver prong settings
- 2 3mm cubic zirconias or other gemstones
- 2 6mm jump rings, 20 gauge
- Pair of earring wires
- Metal clay tool kit

Specialty tools
- Small steel-bristle brush (optional)
- Prong pusher

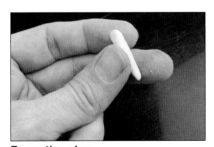

Form the clay
1. Set up your workspace, using an ungreased underlay as the work surface. Pinch off a piece of clay that's about 3 grams and quickly shape it into a little cylinder.

2. Working directly on the underlay, move the ungreased snake roller back and forth over the clay to form a snake about 2mm thick and 4" long with tapered ends. (See sidebar for more details on this technique.)

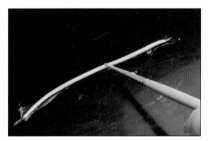

3. Moisten the entire snake with a paintbrush or your finger.

Practice good snake-rolling form

For making clay snakes, it's critical to have the clay in the proper state: not too moist, not too dry (fresh, new clay will still need a bit more water). If you're using scrap clay, moisturize and recondition it so it's fairly soft and totally free of lumps. (See p. 107 for tips on reconditioning scrap clay.) If the clay cracks as you are rolling, it is too dry. Don't simply brush on a bit of water and roll again; the clay will make a slimy mess! Add more water, recondition it, and try rolling again.

Be sure to peel off any protective film that may be on a new roller. Work on an ungreased work surface with an ungreased roller. (By not greasing the tools, you'll have some traction on the clay.) Lightly form the clay into a cylinder with your fingers. Set it on the underlay. Move the snake roller back and forth over the clay with moderate pressure. The pressure is right if the clay gets longer fairly quickly. If you push too hard, the snake will be squashed; not hard enough and it won't grow.

To taper the ends, angle one end of the roller down until it nearly touches the underlay. Continue rolling until the end thins down to a point. Repeat on the other end. Apply a bit of water to all sides of the rope. You've just increased the clay's surface, and it needs more moisture before you work with it.

4. Use a moist paintbrush to push the end of the clay into a spiral, leaving a ⅛" hole at the center of the spiral. Continue coiling the snake until you near the end.

5. Coil the remaining end of the snake in the opposite direction, again leaving a ⅛" hole at the center, until the tip of the clay touches the large spiral. Secure with a bit of paste. The small spiral will be the bail, so be sure that the loop is closed.

6. Use tweezers to press the prong setting into the center of the large spiral, making sure the prongs are sticking up. Press it in until the clay comes up over the lower seat of the setting.

7. Apply syringe clay in the groove around the base of the setting. Smooth the syringe clay with a damp brush.

8. Apply paste to any minor cracks in the spirals. Dry.

9. Repeat steps 1–8, reversing the coiling direction so the pieces mirror each other.

TIP

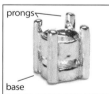

prongs

base

The first time I used a prong setting, I inserted it upside down. This photo should help you. The base gets embedded in the clay; fill the groove around the base with syringe clay.

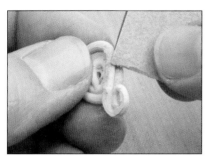

Refine

10. Sand the backs and edges of both pieces to remove any flat spots.

Fire

11. Set the two pieces close together on a firebrick and fire for 3 minutes. Watch the prong settings closely for signs of melting; pull the torch back slightly if they begin to overheat.

Finish and polish

12. Brush all surfaces with a brass-bristle brush. You can use a small steel-bristle brush to get into any tight spots.

Set the stones and assemble

13. Place a gemstone in the setting. I like to use a compass analogy for setting stones: Insert the prong pusher next to the north prong and push it a bit toward the stone. Next, push the south prong, and then the east prong, and finally the west prong.

14. Go back around to each prong again in the same order, pushing a little harder. Repeat until the stone no longer wiggles. Notice that you've bent just the tips of the prongs to secure the stone.

15. Open a jump ring and pass it through the top loop of the earring and an earring wire. Close the jump ring. Repeat steps 13–15 for the second earring.

ANOTHER IDEA

Try making a longer, thicker snake that is tapered only at one end. Coil it up and drill a hole in the large part before it dries. After it's completely dry, you can use a micro carving tool to add lots of texture to it for a totally different look.

PROJECT 7
Simple sparkle earrings

Add some sparkle and color to your metal clay with beautiful cubic zirconias. Learn the basics of setting stones with syringe clay and how to fire CZs and clay together. This technique is very reliable and gives you great practice handling the syringe.

Finished size: 1¼" long

WHAT YOU'LL NEED

Basics
- 7 grams Art Clay Silver 650 or PMC+
- Art Clay Silver 650 Syringe, green tip, or PMC+ Syringe, pink tip
- Pair of earring wires
- 2 or more 3–4mm fireable CZs
- 4 4mm jump rings, 20 gauge
- Metal clay tool kit

Specialty tools
- Rubber stamp sheet
- Straw (2–3mm diameter)
- Small drill bit
- Stone-setting wax (optional)
- Cotton swab
- Rubbing alcohol
- Tweezers
- Fiber blanket
- Bead reamer (optional)
- 2 pairs of flatnose pliers

TIP

The stamp sheet I used for this project has a design of swirls and circles that creates a perfect background for setting gemstones.

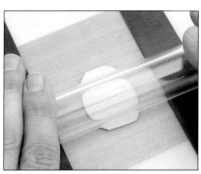

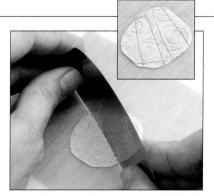

Roll and shape the clay

1. Set up your workspace. Rub a very light coating of olive oil or hand salve on any tools and supplies that will touch the clay. Working quickly, roll all of the clay to 4 cards thick.

2. Texture with the rubber stamp sheet, rolling to 3 cards thick.

3. Use the cutter/scraper or a craft knife to cut two wonky, long rectangles.

 TIP You're not limited to shapes with straight lines. Make any shape you like! You can also use clay cutters to make ovals, circles, or other shapes.

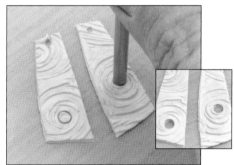

TIP Choose a straw with an opening that's just slightly smaller than your gemstones so the stones won't fall out the back of the earring.

4. Rotate a drill bit into the top of each earring to create a hole at least 3mm from the edge.

5. Use a straw to make holes for the stones: Press the straw down through the clay, give it a quarter turn, and then pull straight up. (I placed the holes at the center of two spirals in the texture.) Recycle the clay plug.

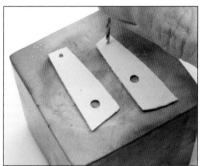

Dry and refine

6. Set the wet pieces aside to dry. After they are completely dry, work on the rubber block and drill gently through the holes again from back to front.

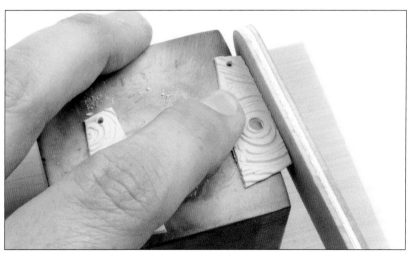

7. Use an emery board to refine the edges and finalize the shapes.

Help for placing tiny stones

To place a tiny stone, you can do the "lick-and-stick" method of licking your finger, touching the flat top (table) of the stone to pick it up, and setting it in place. It is easier and more sanitary to set stones using a product that's made for this purpose such as Embellie Gellie, a scrapbooking product. It is a waxy substance that comes in a handy hinged box. Apply the wax to one end of a stick, pick up the stone, position it in the clay, and use the flat end to press the stone into the clay. I really like this product because it lasts such a long time, and a little goes a long way! Another similar, inexpensive product is made for Bedazzled stones and can be found in the fabric aisle.

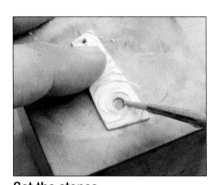

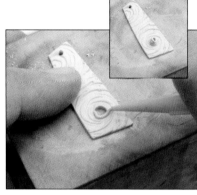

fig. 1

table
girdle

Set the stones

8. Moisten the area around a hole.

9. Use the syringe to make a coiled stack two coils high, starting and stopping in the same location. This creates a coiled bezel setting to hold the stone [**fig. 1**].

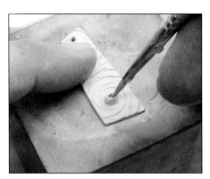

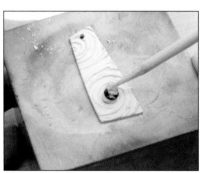

10. Refine the syringe work with a moist brush if necessary.

11. Pick up a tiny bit of stone-setting wax on the pointed tip of the stick.

12. Touch the wax to the flat top (table) of the stone, pick it up, and center it over the coiled setting. Gently set the stone in place.

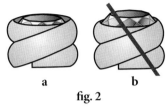

a b

fig. 2

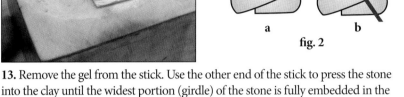

TIP

Never quench stones that are fired in place; they can crack or pop out due to thermal shock.

13. Remove the gel from the stick. Use the other end of the stick to press the stone into the clay until the widest portion (girdle) of the stone is fully embedded in the clay and the flat top (table) is even with or lower than the top of the coiled stack [**fig. 2a**]. Check to be sure the stone is level. **Fig. 2b** shows a stone that has not been pressed in deeply enough; it would pop out as the clay shrinks during firing.

14. Smooth the coiled setting with a moist paintbrush.

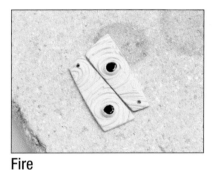

15. Repeat steps 8–14 with the remaining stone for the other earring. Dry. Sand and smooth as necessary. Use a craft knife to scratch off any extra clay on the front and back of both stones.

16. Use a make-up brush to remove any clay dust. Lightly moisten a cotton swab with rubbing alcohol and use it to clean the front and back of each stone. Any residue can permanently fuse to the stone and ruin its sparkle.

Fire

17. Place both pieces as close together as possible on the firebrick. Fire with the torch for 3 minutes, watching carefully so the pieces don't get too hot (overheating can discolor the CZs).

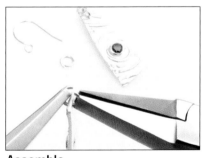

18. After firing, quickly cover both pieces with fiber blanket and set aside to cool. This gradual cooling helps maintain the color of the stones.

Finish and polish

19. Brush with a brass-bristle brush for a satin finish.

Assemble

20. Use a bead reamer to open the holes to accommodate the jump rings, if necessary. Open a jump ring, pick up the earring, and close the ring. Use another jump ring to connect the first jump ring and the earring wire. Repeat with the other earring.

PROJECT 8
Sea urchin bracelet

Making clay snakes with confidence is a skill that every metal clay artisan should have. This project offers great practice in making snakes as a frame for a textured centerpiece. You'll also get practice making consistent syringe bezel settings for fireable CZs. Lots of chain and dangles add the finishing touches.

Finished size: 1x1⅜" centerpiece; 6¾" bracelet

WHAT YOU'LL NEED

Basics
- 10 grams Art Clay Silver 650 or PMC+
- Art Clay Silver 650 Paste or PMC+ Slip
- Art Clay Silver 650 Syringe, green tip, or PMC+ Syringe, pink tip
- 3 3–4mm CZs
- 4 8mm jump rings, 18 gauge
- 7 5mm jump rings, 18 gauge
- 3" sterling silver wire, 24 gauge
- 4' chain
- 2-strand toggle clasp
- 9mm trillion-cut CZ bead
- 2 headpins, 22 gauge
- 2 6mm round crystals
- Assorted beads for dangles
- Metal clay tool kit

Specialty tools & supplies
- Rubber stamp sheet
- Pointed-tip clay shaper
- Snake roller
- Stone-setting wax
- Small straw
- Drill bits
- Cotton swab
- Alcohol
- Fiber blanket
- Bead reamer (optional)
- Chainnose pliers
- Flatnose pliers
- Roundnose pliers
- Flush cutters

Roll and shape the clay

1. Prepare your workspace. Lightly grease all tools and supplies that will touch the clay. Working quickly, roll all of the clay at 5 cards thick into an oval.

2. Flip the clay over and transfer it to the stamp sheet. Texture the clay at 4 cards thick by making one firm roll over the clay. Peel the clay off the stamp. Place the clay textured side up on a nonstick sheet.

3. Apply pressure on the ends of the cutter/scraper to curve it, and use it to trim both long sides of the clay. Trim the short ends in straight lines.

TIP Bracelets take extra abuse, so roll this clay extra-thick for durability.

4. Use a drill bit to make holes at each corner, about 2mm from the edge. You can get close to the edge because the shape will be surrounded by a frame. Remember to apply light pressure to the bit with your index finger while you rotate the bit with your thumb and middle finger.

5. Use a straw that's slightly smaller than the stone to make a hole for each CZ: Press the straw into the clay and rotate a quarter turn. Remember to reclaim the plug of clay from the straw.

Dry and refine

6. Set the wet piece aside to dry. Use an emery board to refine edges and finalize the shape.

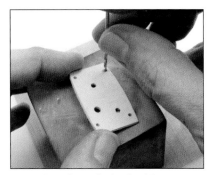

7. Working from the back of the piece, use the drill bit to clean up the small holes.

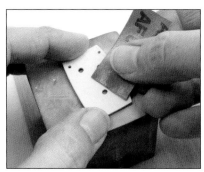

8. Use 600-grit sandpaper to smooth the back.

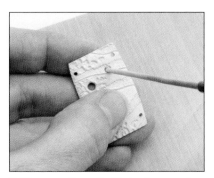

9. Use a small needle file to clean up the straw holes.

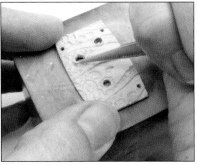

Set the stones

10. Moisten the area around a hole. Use the syringe to make a coiled stack around a hole two coils high, starting and stopping in the same location. Make any necessary adjustments to the syringe work with a moist brush.

11. Pick up a tiny bit of stone-setting wax on the pointed end of the stick. Touch the wax to the flat top (table) of the stone. Gently set the stone in the center of the coiled setting.

12. Remove the wax from the stick and use the flat end of the stick to press the stone into the clay until the widest portion (girdle) of the stone is fully embedded in the clay and level.

13. Use a moist brush to smooth and adjust the syringe bezel if it is wonky.

14. Repeat steps 10–13 with the remaining stones.

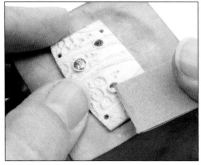

15. Dry completely. Working from the back of the piece, use a craft knife to clean any excess clay from the holes for the stone settings and sand gently as necessary.

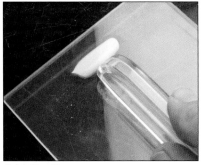

Add the frame

16. Condition and moisturize the excess clay so it's soft and totally free of lumps. Pinch off a pea-sized piece of clay. Working directly on an ungreased underlay, move the snake roller back and forth over the clay to form a long, thin snake about 3mm in diameter.

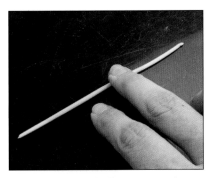

17. Use your finger to apply a bit of water to all sides of the snake. Trim one end at a 45-degree angle. Set aside and cover with plastic wrap.

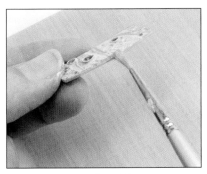

18. Moisten one edge of the centerpiece base.

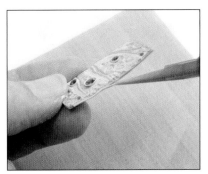

19. Apply a bead of syringe to the moistened edge.

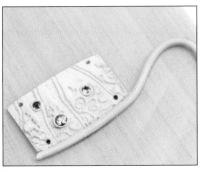

20. Attach the snake to the prepared edge of the centerpiece, placing the cut end at a corner.

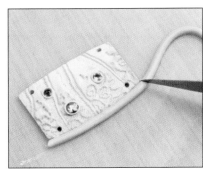

21. Cut the other corner at 45-degree angle.

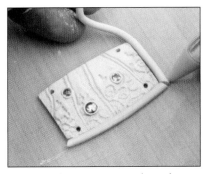

22. Align the remaining snake at the corner, adjusting the mitered corner with a clay shaper. Trim the excess snake at a 45-degree angle.

23. Smooth the corner to eliminate the mitered seam.

TIP

Always make a frame one side at a time with mitered corners that meet perfectly. Don't simply wrap a snake around the corners.

24. Repeat steps 18–23 with the remaining edges to finish the border.

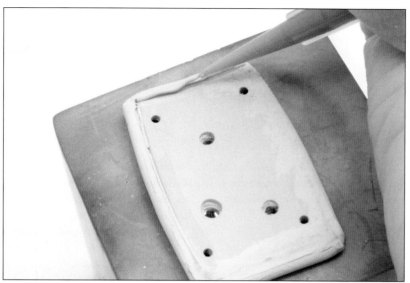

26. Sand the frame flat on all sides. Sand any imperfections so the transition from the base to the frame is smooth.

25. Dry. On the back of the piece, add a line of syringe clay between the frame and the base to fill gaps. Dry completely.

27. Use a make-up brush to remove the clay dust. Moisten a cotton swab with some alcohol and use it to remove any stray clay from the front and back of each stone.

Fire

28. Fire with the torch for 3 minutes, watching closely so the piece does not overheat. Use tweezers to move the fired piece to a fiber blanket to cool slowly to help maintain the stones' color. Do not quench!

Finish and polish

29. Brush with a brass-bristle brush for a satin finish.

30. Use a bead reamer to open the holes enough to accommodate 8mm jump rings, if necessary.

ANOTHER IDEA

For a whimsical look, add texture to the snake frame with a ball-tipped stylus instead of sanding it square. Changing the shape of the stone conveys a very different mood, and a bail is all it takes to transform the frame into a pendant.

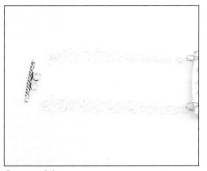
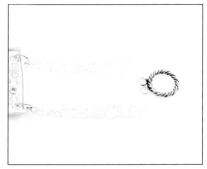

Assemble

31. For a 6¾" bracelet, cut the chain into six 3" pieces and six 2¼" pieces (adjust the lengths of the chain pieces for a different size).

32. On one side of the centerpiece, use 8mm jump rings to connect three chain segments to each hole. Use 5mm jump rings to connect the other ends of the segments to bar end of the toggle.

33. Repeat step 32 on the other side of the centerpiece, but use the shorter chain pieces and the ring end of the toggle.

34. Use the wire to make a wrapped loop for the trillion bead. Make two dangles on headpins using crystals and beads as desired. Attach each dangle with a 5mm jump ring to the chain near the ring end of the toggle.

TIP Because the centerpiece is rather heavy, this bracelet is best worn snug to keep the focal from flipping around the wrist to the back.

Making dangles

Here are a few ways to make dangles that have secure wrapped connections. Place a bead on a headpin, making sure you have at least 1¼" of wire above the bead. Grasp the wire with the tip of your chainnose pliers and make a 45-degree bend just above the bead. Use roundnose pliers to make a basic loop, wrapping the wire end over, down, and around the nose. Wrap the wire end tightly below the loop, coiling two or three times. Trim the excess wire.

To make a dangle from a bead that's drilled from side to side like the trillion bead, center the bead on a 3" (or longer) piece of wire. Bend the wire ends up to meet above the bead. Make a 45-degree bend in one end and wrap it tightly two or three times around the other in a coil. Trim the excess wire.

With the remaining wire, make a basic loop and wrap the end in a tight coil below the loop.

PROJECT 9
Garden links bracelet

Syringe clay can be used for so much more than caulking between two parts—it can be a decorative element by itself. Making these links is great practice for using the syringe to decorate a textured piece of clay for yet another layer of texture and design. The links make lovely focal pieces for this delicate bracelet. You could easily make a matching pair of earrings as well.

Finished size: ⅝x1" center link, 6¼" bracelet

WHAT YOU'LL NEED

Basics
- 10–20 grams Art Clay Silver 650 or PMC+
- Art Clay Silver 650 Syringe, green tip, or PMC+ Syringe, pink tip
- 3 4–6mm firepolished beads
- 6 3mm daisy spacers
- 2 5mm bead caps
- 3 1½" headpins, 22 gauge
- 2 6mm jump rings, 18 gauge
- 4 4mm jump rings, 18 gauge
- 5" sterling silver chain
- Sterling silver toggle
- Metal clay tool kit
- Patina setup

Specialty tools
- Large rubber stamp or stamp sheet
- ¾" oval clay cutter
- ⅝x1⅛" rectangle clay cutter
- Pin vise with 1.5mm (#53) drill bit
- Bead reamer (optional)
- Flatnose pliers
- Chainnose pliers
- Roundnose pliers
- Flush cutters

Roll and shape the clay

1. Prepare your workspace. Lightly grease all tools and supplies that will touch the clay. Working quickly, roll half of the clay to 4 cards thick.

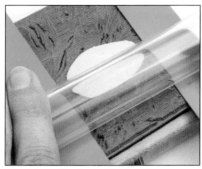

2. Transfer the clay to a greased rubber stamp. Texture the clay at 3 cards thick by making one firm roll over the clay. Remove the textured clay from the stamp. Transfer it design side up to a nonstick sheet.

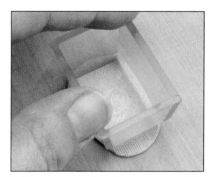

3. Use a rectangular clay cutter to cut the centerpiece shape.

4. Use a drill bit to make holes that are centered on each end and about 3mm from the edge.

5. Roll the remaining clay and texture it in the same way. Use an oval cutter to cut two shapes, and then make holes at each end.

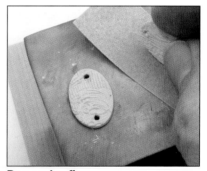

Dry and refine

6. Dry all of the pieces completely. Use sandpaper to refine edges and finalize the shapes. Support the piece on a rubber block as you work. Use the drill bit to open up the holes from the back.

Using syringe clay

If you have done any cake decorating, using syringe clay will probably feel like second nature. If not, read on!

It is very important how you hold the syringe. Resist the temptation to hold the syringe like a doctor, with two fingers under the tabs with a thumb on the plunger. This method will produce very shaky lines. You will have much more control if the syringe is in the palm of the hand with a thumb on the plunger. This way, you can use your wrist to draw with.

Always keep the syringe tip in water when you are not using it. It will dry out in a couple of minutes if it is not moist.

Before using the syringe, wipe off the excess moisture.

Begin by pushing out a tiny bit of clay. Use this to tack the syringe clay to the clay surface. Continue pushing the plunger and lift the syringe tip off the surface about ¼". Let the clay fall into place. Just before you reach the end of the design, stop pressing and then gently touch the syringe to the clay surface and wipe the tip as you would toothpaste. Use a lightly moistened brush to tap down any pointy bits of syringe or to nudge the line into place if it isn't exactly where you want it.

Embellish

7. Lightly moisten the areas where you will apply the syringe clay.

8. Apply swirling details (I followed lines in my texture). Smooth any undesired points with a damp brush.

9. If the syringe work does not seem well attached, apply a drop of water to the tip of the paintbrush and touch it to the connection point. The water will wick under the syringe clay detail and help it stick better. (Don't get carried away or you will dissolve your design.)

10. After about a minute, press gently with your index finger to ensure a good connection.

11. Rotate between the three components as you embellish to give the syringe work a chance to dry. This will also make it less likely that you accidentally squash a beautiful element that you just perfected. Dry completely.

Fire

12. Place all three links as close together as possible on the firebrick, almost touching. Because the pieces are small and can fit together in a space the size of a half dollar, you can fire them together. Fire for 3 minutes. Pick up the brick from the sides and slide the pieces into a bowl of water to quench.

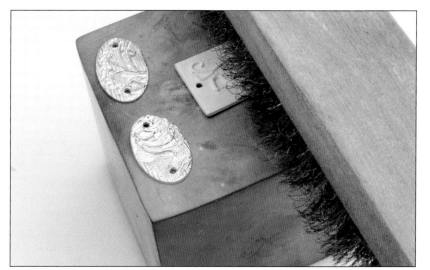

Finish and polish

13. Brush with a brass-bristle brush.

14. Using tweezers, dip each piece into a liver of sulfur solution until darkened.

15. Rinse, dry, and use a polishing cloth on each.

Assemble the bracelet

16. Make three wire-wrapped dangles as shown using the headpins, the firepolished crystals, the daisy spacers, and the bead caps.

TIP

I never do a final trim of the chain until I have tried on a bracelet or necklace. Give yourself some wiggle room!

17. Use 6mm jump rings to connect the links. If the holes are too tight for the rings to pass through, use a bead reamer to open each hole a bit.

18. Cut two 2–2½" pieces of chain (adjust to your wrist size). Use 4mm rings to connect the chains to each side of the centerpiece.

19. Open a jump ring and pick up the dangles, the toggle loop, and the end link of chain. Close the jump ring.

20. Use a 4mm ring to connect the remaining chain ends to the toggle bar. If necessary, reposition the toggle bar on the chain until the bracelet fits well, and then trim the excess chain.

PROJECT10
Fairy Hollow necklace

These delicate links of curling tendrils are accented with leaves and a lighter-than-air leaf focal piece. Practice carving your own tips for new decorative possibilities with the syringe. Also make your own oval jump rings to link the vines together into a very feminine design.

Finished size: 1⅝" pendant, 18½" necklace

WHAT YOU'LL NEED

Basics
- 30 grams Art Clay Silver 650 Syringe with gray, green, and blue tips or PMC+ Syringe with olive, pink, and blue tips
- 7 grams Art Clay Silver 650 or PMC+
- 2' sterling silver wire, 20 gauge, dead soft
- Clasp
- Metal clay tool kit

Specialty tools
- Ultra-flush wire cutters
- 2x5mm rectangular mandrel (I used a flat barbeque skewer)
- V-cut carving tool
- Bamboo skewer
- Wedge-tip clay shaper or toothpick
- ³⁄₁₆" and ⁵⁄₁₆" teardrop clay cutters
- 2 4x4" smooth, glazed tiles
- Tumbler (optional)

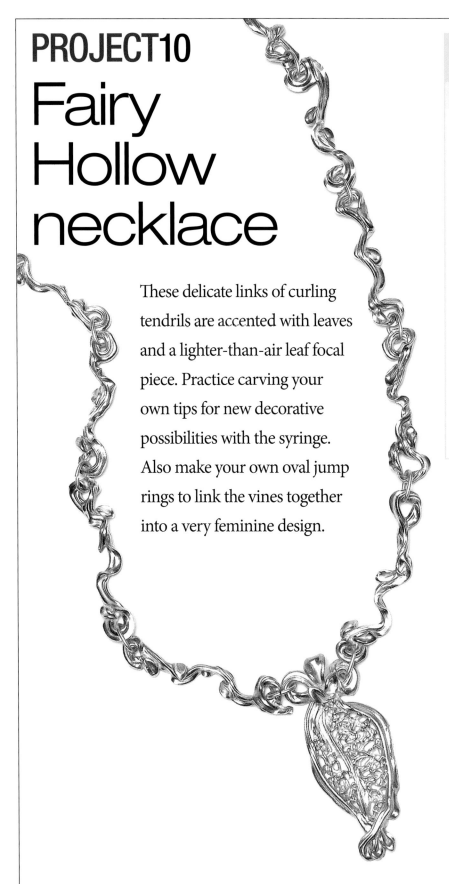

pattern

Shape the links

1. Photocopy or trace the pattern. Trim the paper copy to fit on a tile. Cover the tile with a nonstick sheet and firmly tape it in place, leaving one side untaped so you can slide the pattern copy in and move it around. Do not grease the nonstick sheet. Set aside.

TIP The tile keeps the delicate syringe work intact as you work and makes it easy to transfer the work in and out of the drying environment.

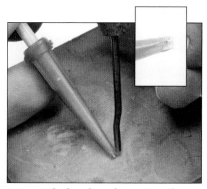

2. Insert the bamboo skewer into the large syringe tip. (The skewer will support the tip as you carve.) Support the tip on the rubber block and use the carving tool to cut six V-shaped grooves around the end of the tip. (Think of making the Vs at the points of a clock in this order: 12, 6, 10, 4, 2, 8.) This will make a star-shaped tip. Don't cut off any length from the tip or the extrusion will be too wide. Put this tip on the syringe dispenser.

Make the links

3. Use the syringe with the star-shaped tip to "draw" in clay over the link pattern. As you draw, twist the syringe a bit and apply varying pressure to add interest to the links. Be sure the loops on each end are closed and that the holes made by the loops are large enough to allow a jump ring through. Use a moist paintbrush to tap down any pointy bits of clay formed while starting or stopping and to nudge any stray syringe lines into position.

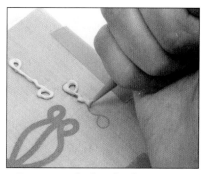

4. Drawing in freehand style, create 17 more links of similar size, making each a little bit different. Switch to another set of nonstick sheet and tile if necessary. Touch up with a moist brush, if necessary, and set all of the links aside to dry on the tile(s). Reinforce any questionable connections with small amounts of syringe clay and dry again.

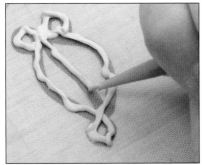

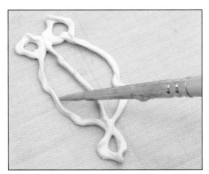

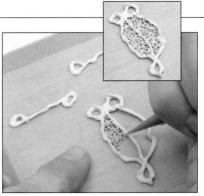

Make the focal pendant

5. Using the pattern under a nonstick sheet, create the outline of the focal pendant in one continuous extrusion, and then add the center vein. Dry.

6. Switch to the fine syringe tip. Wrap the star-shaped tip in a wet paper towel as you work with the fine tip. Moisten the inside perimeter of the leaf with a moist brush.

7. Fill in the leaf with squiggles of syringe clay. Make sure the squiggles are interconnected and well connected to the outline. Lightly tap down any stray squiggles with the brush. Dry.

Add leaf embellishments

8. Roll a small amount of lump clay 2 cards thick. Use both cutters to cut a few leaf shapes. Store the excess clay and keep the shapes covered with plastic as you work.

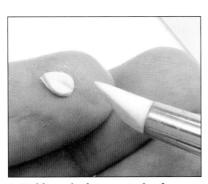

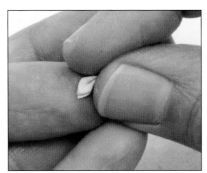

TIP

It's OK to store the syringe tip down in a cup of water between project steps.

9. Holding a leaf on your index finger, use the clay shaper or the end of a toothpick to impress a vein at the rounded end.

10. Pinch the sides together at that end to make a leaf shape. Set aside to dry. Continue to shape leaves and roll additional clay to make more until you have 30 small and 5 large leaves. Dry. Sand each leaf a bit.

11. Place the medium tip on the syringe and wrap the fine tip in a wet paper towel. Use syringe clay to attach the leaves to the links in random ways.

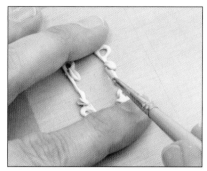

12. Smooth the ooze as you go.

13. Place at least one large and two small leaves at the top of the focal pendant. Dry.

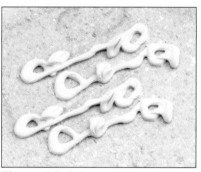

Fire and finish

14. Place several dried pieces as close together as possible on the firebrick. (You should be able to fire up to four links at a time.) Fire for 3 minutes. Let the pieces cool naturally on the brick. Repeat until all the links are fired. Fire the pendant separately. Do not quench any of the pieces; pieces with lots of connected elements can pop apart.

15. Brush the pieces with a brass-bristle brush. For extra shine and surface durability, you can tumble after brushing.

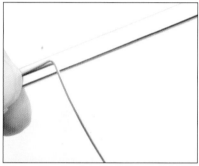

Make the jump rings

16. Bend ¾" of the wire at a 90-degree angle. Hold this end of the wire firmly along the flat barbecue skewer (a good mandrel for making oval jump rings).

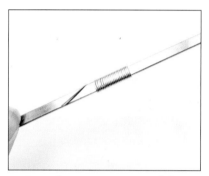

17. Wrap the remaining wire tightly around the mandrel to form an oval coil. Slide the coil off the mandrel.

TIP

Make flush cuts in wire for secure links and a professional look. Wire cutters produce two very different surfaces as wire is cut. The end next to the flat side of the cutters will have a clean, straight cut. The other end will have a bur—a pinched, rough cut. Because of this, place the flat side of the cutters toward the ring and trim the rough wire end after every cut.

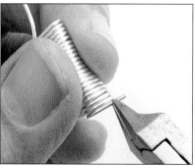

18. Flush-cut the coil to make rings: Pull the coil apart so you have a slight space between each ring. Trim the end of the wire, placing the flat side of the cutters toward the coil.

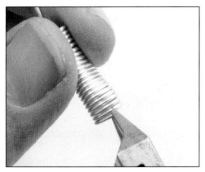

19. Flip the cutters over, aligning the flat side with the cut you just made. Cut. You made a ring.

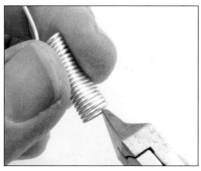

20. Flip the pliers again and trim the bur. Flip the pliers and align the flat side with the cut you just made. Cut. You made another ring.

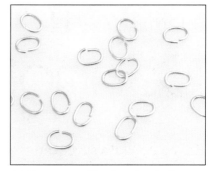

21. Repeat step 20, trimming the bur after each cut. Make sure the cuts are always on the straight portion of the rings. If the cuts get too close to the curve, trim off the curve and continue.

ANOTHER IDEA

This lightweight filigree is terrific as a pair of earrings and uses the exact same techniques. Just make three loops at the bottom to hang some sparking crystals, and a loop at the top to attach the earring wire!

Assemble

22. Arrange the links in pairs of similar length. Lay out the pairs to create the left and right sides of the necklace. Use the jump rings to connect the links. Each side will connect to one side of the pendant. The loop at the bottom can be used to dangle additional goodies. Use jump rings to attach a clasp at the back.

PROJECT 11
Cannoli slider

Rolled up like a silver cannoli, this fun-to-make slider pendant is quick, easy, and versatile. Because the pendant has a large hole, you can easily move it to another cord or chain for a different look. You can make different sizes by forming around various things: drinking straws, boba straws, milkshake straws, even tubes that seed beads are packaged in. Keep your eyes open for all the many possibilities out there!

Finished width: ⅝"

WHAT YOU'LL NEED

Basics
- 10 grams Art Clay Silver 650 or PMC+
- Art Clay Silver 650 Paste or PMC+ Slip
- Art Clay Silver 650 Syringe, green tip, or PMC+ Syringe, pink tip
- Metal clay tool kit
- Patina setup (optional)

Specialty tools
- Rubber stamp
- Seed bead tube, 15mm diameter
- Pointed-tip clay shaper
- Snake roller

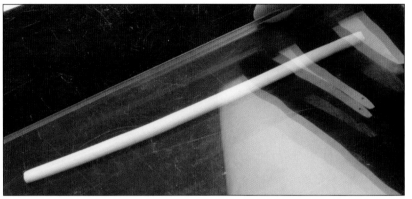

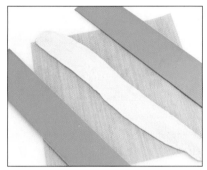

Roll and shape the clay

1. Set up your workspace. Lightly grease all tools and supplies that will touch the clay except the underlay and snake roller. With your hands, quickly shape the clay into a cylinder. Working on the ungreased underlay, use the snake roller to form a snake about 4mm in diameter. Give it a little squash with the snake roller to flatten it a bit.

2. Transfer the squashed snake to a greased nonstick sheet. Roll the snake to 3 cards thick and about 6" long.

You can use the pattern on the right as a guide: Photocopy or trace the shape and place the copy under the nonstick sheet before you begin.

3. Transfer the clay to a greased stamp. Set 2-card-thick slats on both sides of the clay on top of the stamp. Roll the clay firmly once.

4. Transfer the clay to the nonstick sheet. Trim one short end straight. Trim the two long edges straight and parallel.

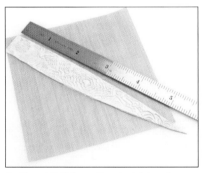

5. About 2¼" from the straight end, angle the blade so the sides meet in a sharp point.

6. Starting with the wide end of the shape, wrap the clay around the greased bead tube, working near the open end of the tube. Lift up the pointed tip gently and apply paste to the textured clay underneath, covering an area from the tip and about ½" upward.

7. Gently press the tip back into place. Hold it briefly with the clay shaper to seal the seam. Smooth any ooze with a damp brush.

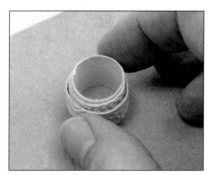

Dry and refine

8. Set the slider aside to dry completely. Gently remove the slider from the tube by twisting it back and forth as you slide it off the end. Cut a small, square piece of 180-grit sandpaper. Without squeezing the shape, smooth the sides flat using a circular motion.

Fire

9. Set the slider on its side on the firebrick. This will prevent flattening of the cylinder during firing. Fire for 4 minutes. Cool naturally.

Finish and polish

10. Brush with a brass-bristle brush. Using tweezers, dip into a warm liver of sulfur solution until you see a patina you like. Rinse and dry. Use a polishing cloth on the inside, if needed, but not on the outside.

pattern

ANOTHER IDEA

The same slider can easily be transformed into a bead by adding smooth, domed ends that fit the diameter of the cannoli tube. After the ends are dry, sand them and use syringe clay to attach them to the tube. I like to give the ends a shiny finish, which is a nice contrast to the textured cylinder. For this bracelet, I made two small and one large cannoli bead and then simply strung them with some amazonite rondelles.

PROJECT 12
Hollow lentil beads

Create beautiful domed, hollow beads with clay textured by embossing. Brass dies give the clay an entirely different look than rubber stamps; the design will be raised with really crisp, straight edges instead of depressed into the clay with soft edges. The domed halves fit perfectly together to make self-supporting lentil beads with holes on the sides.

Finished diameters: 1", ½"

WHAT YOU'LL NEED

Basics
- 20 grams Art Clay Silver 650 or PMC+
- Art Clay Silver 650 Paste or PMC+Slip
- Art Clay Silver 650 Syringe, green tip, or PMC+ Syringe, pink tip
- Aluminum foil
- Metal clay tool kit

Specialty tools
- Brass embossing dies
- 1½ –1¾" small round appliance light bulbs or ping pong balls (2 of the same size)
- Marbles (4 of the same size)
- 1⅛" and ⅝" circle cutters
- Micro round needle file
- Drill bit

Prepare the forms
1. Cut a piece of aluminum foil to about 6x6", fold it in half, and wrap it around the base of the light bulb, leaving about 1" of foil extending below the base of the bulb.

TIP Metal clay should never come in contact with aluminum of any sort. The metals will react with each other and ruin the silver, so be sure that when you set the clay-covered marble in place it doesn't touch the foil.

2. Squash the loose foil down to make a flared base to hold the bulb upright.

Repeat steps 1–2 with a second bulb and piece of foil.

3. For the smaller bead forms, make a foil boat to support the marbles by folding a 6x12" strip of foil into a 1x12" strip. Set a marble on the foil about 2" from an end. Pinch the foil about halfway up the marble to hold it securely. Repeat down the length of the foil to secure four marbles. Flatten the ends a bit to make tabs to hold.

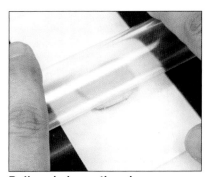

Roll and shape the clay
4. Set up your workspace. Lightly grease any tools and supplies that will touch the clay, including the brass die and the light bulbs or ping pong balls. Working quickly, roll 5 grams of clay to 4 cards thick.

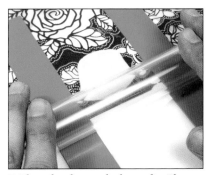

5. Place the clay on the brass die. Place 3-card-thick slats or stacks on both sides of the clay and on top of the die. Roll firmly once.

6. Using a 1⅛" cutter, cut one disk.

7. Drape the disk over the prepared light bulb. Gently press the disk down first at the north and south points, and then move to east and west. This will help shape the clay to the form evenly.

TIP

Brass dies are different from rubber stamps in two key ways. First, they give a really crisp image because they are made from cut metal. Second, and most importantly, the design is raised above the surface of the clay. It is a beautiful, refined look.

8. Use all your fingers to ease the entire edge down at the same time until it fits the contour of the bulb. The clay will tend to pop up on one side as you press the other, so the more fingers you use, the easier it will be.

9. The entire disk should touch the bulb. If you have any puckers, the bead pieces will not fit together correctly. If you can't get it, remove the clay, recondition it, and start over (I promise that will really be faster in the end!). See p. 107 for more on reconditioning clay.

See p. 107 for more on reconditioning clay.

10. Roll another 5 grams of clay and repeat steps 4–9.

11. For the small beads, roll out 2.5 grams of clay. Repeat steps 4–9 four times, except use a ⅝" cutter and drape the clay disks over a marble in the foil holder, making sure the clay does not touch the aluminum.

Dry and refine

12. Dry completely. When placed together, the two bead halves won't line up perfectly because of the thickness of the clay.

13. To make the halves fit nicely, sand the edge of one half-dome completely flat by moving it in a circular motion on a sheet of 180-grit sandpaper. Repeat with the second half-dome.

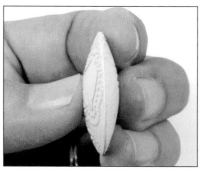

14. Check the fit and adjust until the bead halves align perfectly.

Make the holes

15. On one half-dome, mark a hole position with a pencil. For the large bead, position the holes above the centerline so the bead will not flip around as it is worn.

You can make
decorative bead caps by forming half a lentil bead, punching out tiny decorative shapes, and drilling a hole in the middle.

16. Put the two halves together and transfer the marks to the second half-dome.

17. Transfer the marks to the inside of each half.

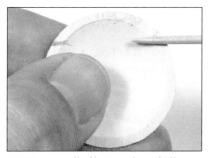

18. Use a needle file to make a shallow pilot hole on each side of one half-dome. Don't file too much. Point the tip of the file directly toward the mark on the opposite side of the bead.

Repeat on the opposite side and for the second half-dome.

Assemble

19. Moisten the sanded edge of each half with a damp brush.

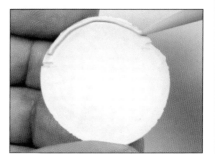

20. Run a bead of syringe clay around the edge of one dome, avoiding the pilot holes.

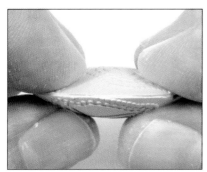

21. Gently but firmly press the two halves together, making sure the pilot holes line up. Dry. Sand any rough edges.

22. Repeat steps 12–21 to create two small beads, except place the pilot holes at the centerlines of the disks in step 15.

23. Insert the drill bit into the pilot hole. Without pushing too hard, turn the bit clockwise to shave away the clay and make a clean hole. Repeat on the other side. Add a bit of syringe clay around the hole if you see any gaps.

ANOTHER IDEA

For a lentil pendant, make just one dome. Use a larger (1½") cutter and make the hanging hole with a straw. Fire it with the flat side down to keep its shape. Add a ribbon and it's ready to wear!

Fire

24. Place the large bead on the firebrick and support it with bits of fiber blanket around the edges to help maintain its domed shape. Fire the large bead by itself for 3 minutes. Place both small beads on the brick, add small bits of fiber blanket, and fire together for 3 minutes. Cool naturally; the temperature shock of quenching can pop the seams.

Finish and polish

25. Create the finish of your choice. I brushed my beads with a steel-bristle brush for a scratch finish.

PROJECT**13**
Crossover ring

Making your own rings is one of the most satisfying things you can do with metal clay. This ring is a great version for beginners because you don't have to worry about the seam. Because the clay shrinks a bit, pay attention to the tips about sizing: You have to make the ring a bit larger to compensate for the clay's shrinkage during firing.

Finished width of band: ⅛"

WHAT YOU'LL NEED

Basics
- 10 grams Art Clay Silver 650 or PMC+
- Art Clay Silver 650 Paste or PMC+ Slip
- Aluminum foil
- Metal clay tool kit

Specialty tools
- Ring sizer (optional)
- Nonstick ring strip or sticky note
- Ring mandrel, preferably stepped
- Pointed-tip clay shaper
- Large sanding swabs (optional)
- Small steel-bristle brush
- Tumbler (optional)

Prepare the mandrel

1. If you don't know the desired ring size, use a sizer to measure it. For this style and width of band (4–10mm wide), you'll need to increase the working size by 1½ sizes. For example, a finished size 7 ring needs to be formed as a size 8½.

2. Wrap a strip of nonstick sheet around a ring mandrel. (You can also use a sticky note with the sticky side out so it sticks to itself, not the mandrel.) Tape the nonstick strip together with a slim strip of clear tape just along just the ends. Grease the nonstick strip and set the mandrel aside.

Mandrel types
There are two styles of mandrel: tapered and stepped. A tapered mandrel is smooth and cone shaped with the sizes engraved into it. A stepped mandrel has an even, not tapered, surface for each size. Stepped mandrels are easiest to deal with when you are making metal clay rings. They give you a wide area that is a consistent size, and this will help ensure that the ring will end up being the size you want it to be.

3. Check the approximate length of clay needed by wrapping a scrap of paper around the nonstick strip and make a pencil mark. Make another mark about 1" past the first mark. This will give you a rough estimate of how long the clay strip will need to be.

Ring shaping and sizing

Sizing is key when making rings. Because the clay shrinks about 10% during firing, you have to make the ring a bit larger than the desired finished size. Thickness, width, and size all affect the amount of shrinkage of a ring. It can get a bit complicated, so let's start at the beginning. This basic ring needs to be made about 1½ sizes bigger than the desired finished size.

If you need to make a half-size ring, and have only a full-size mandrel, wrap the nonstick sheet around the mandrel one extra time. The addition of this thin sheet will make the ring about a half size bigger. It is amazing how similar ring sizes really are!

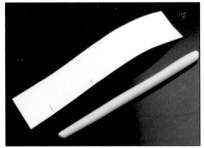

Roll and shape the ring

4. Set up your workspace. Lightly grease your hands and a nonstick sheet. On an ungreased underlay, roll the of clay into a snake that reaches the second mark on your paper guide, usually about 3½" long.

5. Squash the snake a bit with the snake roller to flatten it.

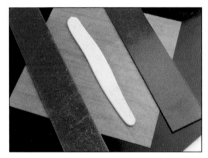

6. Transfer the clay to the nonstick sheet and roll to 6 cards thick. If the clay seems dry, brush it with water and cover it with plastic for a short time to hydrate.

7. Trim the clay to the desired width, creating a taper of about ⅛–¼". Using the second mark as a guide, trim the narrow end of clay strip.

8. Starting with the narrow end, wrap the clay strip around the prepared mandrel. Continue wrapping the wide end over the top of the narrow end. Lift the wide end and trim off some of the narrow end, leaving about ¼" of overlap.

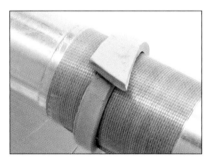

9. Apply paste to the narrow end where the wide end will overlap. Set the wide end back in place, curving it down a bit so the top of the ring is flat. (This will be important for the firing stage.) Press in place and hold for a few seconds.

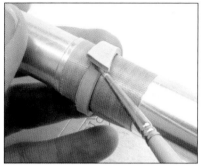

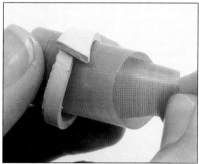

10. Smooth the seam with a moist paintbrush.

Dry and refine

11. If your mandrel does not have a stand, prop the narrow end of the mandrel on a wad of foil. Leave the ring on the mandrel to dry. As soon as the ring is dry to the touch (about 10 minutes without heat), carefully slide the nonstick strip and the ring off the mandrel.

12. Remove all tape. Use tweezers or your fingers to very carefully grab the inner edge of nonstick sheet and coil it inward to remove it from the ring. Apply more paste to the seam inside. Dry completely. Add more paste if necessary, dry, and repeat until the seam is smooth.

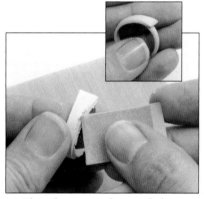

13. Place the ring on the mandrel (wrapped with a nonstick sheet if the mandrel is aluminum) or support it with your fingers. Catch the clay dust with a sheet of paper. Use 180-grit sandpaper to refine the edges and finalize the shape. Thin the end of the wedge to remove some bulk from the ring and taper the edges of the band for a refined look.

14. Sand the inside of the ring (a sanding swab works well for this). Make the seam inside totally smooth.

ANOTHER IDEA

Use the same crossover technique

to make a ribbon to show your support of a loved one with an illness. Instead of forming a ring, loop the clay around and cross the ends. A single initial is enough to personalize this meaningful charm. I applied a patina to half of the ribbon to symbolize the darkness of the cancer my friend faces, but left the other side bright as symbol of hope. (Keep up the fight, Kathy!)

15. Place the ring on the firebrick, flat side down. Rings get extra strength from longer sintering, so fire for 5 minutes, holding the color so it looks closer to hot lava than peach. Watch closely so the ring does not melt. Cool.

Finish and polish

16. Brush with a brass-bristle brush. Use a small steel-bristle brush on the inside.

PROJECT 14
Twisted ring

This is the next step in acquiring ring-making skills: learning how to make a seamless join. The twist is a great design element that will give you practice in properly conditioning clay.

Finished width of band: ⁵⁄₁₆"

WHAT YOU'LL NEED

Basics
- 10 grams Art Clay Silver 650 or PMC+
- Art Clay Silver 650 Syringe, green tip, or PMC+ Slip
- Aluminum foil
- Metal clay tool kit

Specialty tools
- Nonstick ring strip or sticky note
- Ring mandrel, preferably stepped
- Clay shaper
- Large sanding swabs (optional)
- Small steel-bristle brush
- Rubber mallet (optional)
- Tumbler (optional)

See the previous ring project for more tips on ring sizing.

TIP

The more things you plan to do to the clay, the more moisture it needs to make it through without cracking. Because you will be rolling, twisting, and wrapping this clay, it needs to be pretty moist. Moisturize the clay by adding a few drops of water. Work it in. It should give easily when pressed without being sticky.

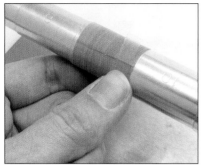

Prepare the mandrel

1. Establish the desired ring size. The working size for a 5–10mm wide ring like this is 1½ sizes larger. Wrap a strip of nonstick sheet (or a sticky note with sticky side out) around a ring mandrel. Tape the nonstick strip to itself with a narrow strip of clear tape along the ends.

2. Check the approximate length of clay needed by wrapping a scrap of paper around the nonstick strip and making a pencil mark where it overlaps. Make another mark about 1" beyond the first mark to indicate the length of the clay strip.

Roll and shape the ring

3. Set up your workspace. Lightly grease your hands and a nonstick sheet. On an ungreased underlay, roll the clay into a snake that reaches the first mark on your guide, usually about 3" long.

4. Squash the clay with the snake roller to flatten it a bit.

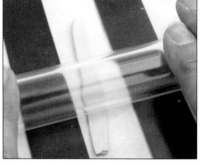

5. Transfer the clay to the nonstick sheet. Roll the strip 4 cards thick. If the strip is dry, brush it with water and cover it with plastic for a short time.

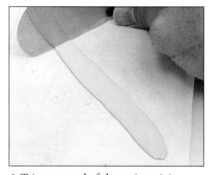

6. Trim one end of clay strip so it is straight.

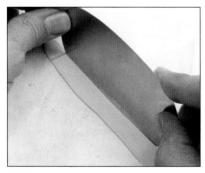

7. Trim the strip to the desired width, keeping in mind that the wider the band is, the taller the finished ring will be—don't go too crazy!

8. Be sure the clay strip reaches the second mark on the paper. If it does not, gather up all the clay, condition it, and start at step 3 again, making the strip slightly narrower.

9. Twist the clay near the trimmed end. (You may need to thin the clay in the twisted area to get the clay to twist well.)

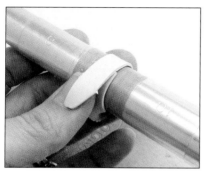

10. Keeping the twist in the clay, wrap the clay strip around the prepared mandrel. Lay the trimmed end down first. Wrap the other end over the trimmed end.

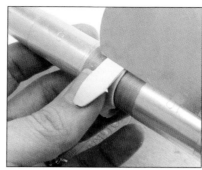

11. With the cutter at a 45-degree (or greater) angle, trim through both layers of the ring. Remove both pieces of excess clay.

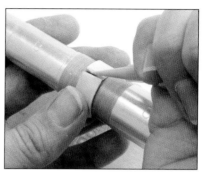

12. Apply a bead of syringe clay along the seam.

13. Firmly blend and smooth the syringe clay into the seam with the clay shaper.

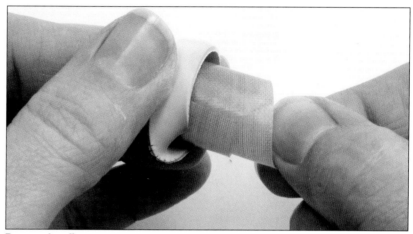

Dry and refine

14. If your mandrel does not have a stand, prop the narrow end of mandrel on a wad of foil. As soon as the ring is dry to the touch (about 10 minutes without heat), carefully slide the nonstick sheet and the ring off the mandrel. The ring should not be totally dry; removing it early will prevent the seam from pulling apart as the clay continues to shrink as it dries. Dry 10 minutes with heat.

Remove all tape. Use tweezers or your fingers to very carefully grab the inner edge of the nonstick sheet and coil it inward to remove it from the ring.

15. Apply more syringe to the seam, inside and out. Dry fully and repeat until the connection is solid and the seam is smooth.

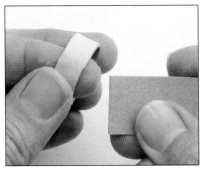

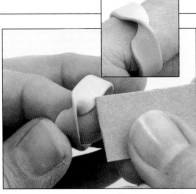

16. Place the ring back on the mandrel (wrapped with nonstick sheet if the mandrel is aluminum) or fully support it with your fingers while sanding. Place a sheet of paper underneath to catch sanding dust. Use 180-grit sandpaper to refine the seam and finalize the shape. Sand the inside of the ring as well (a sanding swab works well for this).

17. Repeat steps 15–16 if any part of the seam is visible. Dry the ring completely.

18. Go over the entire ring with finer sandpaper to remove sanding scratches. Band rings are more comfortable if they have slightly rounded edges. Run sandpaper along the cut edges until they are beveled. Continue sanding the edges until they are smooth and rounded.

19. Place the ring on the firebrick. Rings get extra strength from longer sintering, so fire for 5 minutes, holding the color so it looks closer to hot lava than peach. Watch closely so the ring does not melt. Cool.

20. If firing distorted the ring shape a bit, place it back on the ring mandrel and gently hit the ring with a rubber mallet to smooth the flat band.

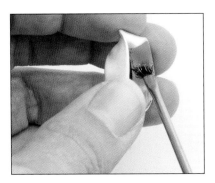

Finish

21. Brush with a brass-bristle brush. Use a small steel-bristle brush on the inside of the band.

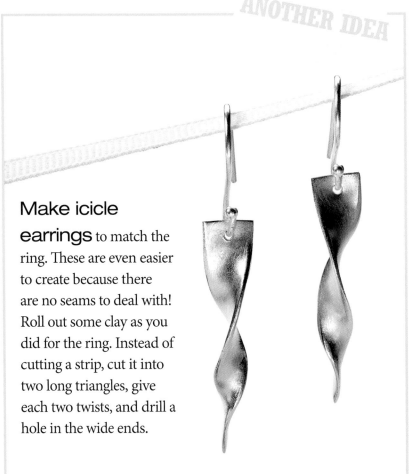

ANOTHER IDEA

Make icicle earrings to match the ring. These are even easier to create because there are no seams to deal with! Roll out some clay as you did for the ring. Instead of cutting a strip, cut it into two long triangles, give each two twists, and drill a hole in the wide ends.

PROJECT 15
Nature's beauty earrings

Use clay in its paste form to capture delicate natural forms forever in silver. This technique is wonderful because even the smallest details are visible in the finished pieces. Feathers are so fragile…this transformation makes them eternal. Choose a pleasant day for firing this project— you'll do that step outdoors.

Finished length: 1¾"

WHAT YOU'LL NEED

Basics
- 10 grams Art Clay Silver 650 Paste or PMC+ Slip
- 2 1½"-long leaves or feathers
- 2 fine-silver screw eyes
- Pair of earring wires
- Metal clay tool kit

Specialty tools
- Press'n Seal plastic wrap
- 4x4" smooth, glazed tile
- Metal file

Prepare the tile
1. Seal the plastic wrap tightly around the tile with the sticky side up. Tape it in place on the back.

2. Set the feathers on the tile wrong side up, pressing them so they stick to the plastic wrap. The tile will help support the fragile feathers as you work.

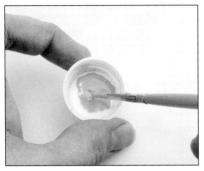

Paint and dry

3. Thin about ¼ teaspoon of paste to a milk-like consistency. (I used the paste cap to do this.) Stir gently to prevent bubbles. This thin consistency will ensure that the clay flows into every nook and cranny to capture all of the details.

4. Using a paintbrush with a fine, pointed tip, paint a layer of thin paste on the feathers. Paint with the grain of each feather and don't go outside the lines; keep all the paste on the feather.

Do not go over an area with more paste until it is fully dry (when the entire surface changes from gray to white). This layer is not dry; notice the gray spots. Set aside to dry for a few minutes. Do not put in a heated dryer yet, or the feathers will curl too much.

5. Apply another thin layer with a flat brush. Set aside to dry. Make sure that each layer is completely dry before applying the next or you will pull off chunks of clay.

TIP Glad Press'n Seal is designed for wrapping food, but its tacky qualities are terrific for this project. It will help prevent the feathers from moving around while you are painting and minimize curling at the edges as the paste dries.

6. Continue to apply more layers using thicker paste each time and setting aside to dry between applications. After applying about five layers, you can begin to introduce heat to dry the clay, which will speed up the process.

ANOTHER IDEA

Use a leaf instead
of feathers. Select a thin leaf that has prominent veining and no fuzz on the underside; avoid thick, meaty leaves. Paint paste on the back of the leaf where the veins are most prominent. The back of the leaf will become the front of the pendant. I finished this pendant with two thin snakes of clay twisted together as a bail.

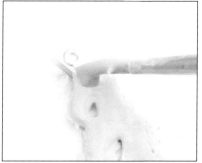

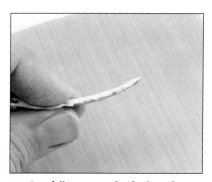

7. Use tweezers to set a screw eye at the top of each earring so the loop is at the top.

8. Add paste at the point where the screw is embedded.

9. Continue adding more layers of paste to the entire feather. You should end up applying about 10 layers; you'll probably use up most of the jar of paste. Your results may vary; don't worry. Your goal is a layer of paste at least 1mm thick, not including the feather.

10. Carefully remove the feathers from the plastic wrap. Check the thickness and add more paste if necessary. Clean up any stray paste on the front of the feathers by gently scraping it off.

TIP Do the "mirror check" if you're not sure whether the feathers are dry: Set them on a mirror for 30 seconds. If you pick them up and see fog left behind, dry them more.

Fire

11. Be sure the both pieces are completely dry before firing. Be extra cautious with these because it is really easy to have trapped moisture within all the layers of paste.

12. Set the feathers as close as possible on a firebrick, almost touching. Fire outdoors for 4 minutes. As the feathers burn off, they'll produce extra smoke and a longer-burning flame. (If you ever use this technique with a larger feather, fire it by itself.) Quench to cool.

Finish and polish

13. Brush the feathers with a brass-bristle brush for a satin finish.

14. Use a metal file to smooth any rough edges. Attach each feather to an earring wire with a jump ring.

TIP Small, thin things like feathers and delicate leaves can be successfully torch-fired like this, but do not use this technique on large or thick objects. Torch-firing bulky items produces a lot more flame and smoke; the silver can overheat and melt. Burning away organic items is typically done in a kiln, and for many items, it is the best way to fire. When fired in the kiln, consumables will smolder rather then burn.

PROJECT 16
Pea-in-the-pod pendant

This elegant pendant features a delicate pearl nestled into a pod of silver. Pearls cannot be fired, but fine silver wire can be. Build a piece of wire into the clay that you can later use to mount a half-drilled pearl. Two contrasting textures inside and out complete the look. This project is a great skill-builder because you will be doing lots of manipulation of wet clay.

Finished length: 1⅞"

WHAT YOU'LL NEED

Basics
- 10 grams Art Clay Silver 650 or PMC+
- Art Clay Silver 650 Syringe, green tip, or PMC+ Syringe, pink tip
- ½" fine-silver wire, 20 gauge
- 6mm half-drilled pearl
- Metal clay tool kit

Specialty tools
- Freezer paper
- Bead reamer (optional)
- Cutting mat
- Snake roller
- Small steel-bristle brush
- Chainnose pliers
- Flush cutter
- G-S Hypo jewelry cement
- Wet/dry sandpaper: 600, 1200, and 2000 grit

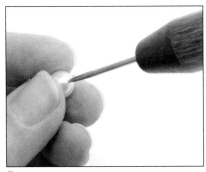

Prepare
1. Make sure the 20-gauge wire fits into the pearl. If not, use the bead reamer to enlarge the pearl's hole a bit.

TIP Whenever you insert something like wire or a fine-silver finding into clay, make sure it has a rough surface. This will give the clay something to hold on to as it shrinks. Commercial findings often have notches that provide this grab. Without adding a few "bites" from the pliers, super-slick wire will pull right out later.

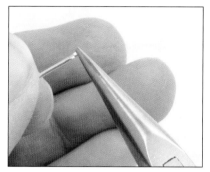

2. Use chainnose pliers to mar one end of the wire; this will help the clay grab the wire as it dries and sinters.

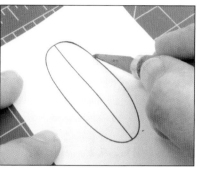

3. Photocopy or trace the pattern. Cut around the outline using a craft knife on a self-healing mat. Grease the back of the pattern copy.

Roll and shape the clay

4. Set up your workspace. Cover an underlay with a piece of greased freezer paper. Lightly grease any other tools and supplies that will touch the clay. Working quickly, roll all of the clay to 4 cards thick and slightly larger than the pattern.

TIP Freezer paper makes a great nonstick surface because it's inexpensive and doesn't have any unwanted texture. I always use freezer paper when sanding is going to be a challenge or if I know I need an extra-smooth surface.

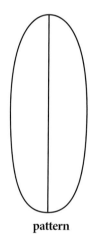

pattern

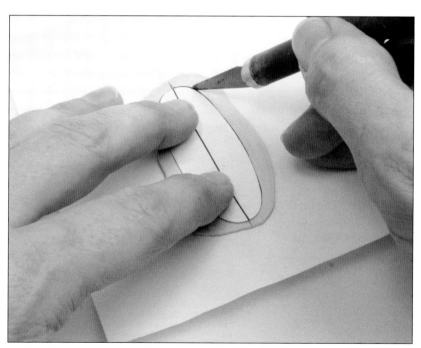

5. Place the pattern greased side down on the rolled clay. Trim around the outline. Remove the pattern copy.

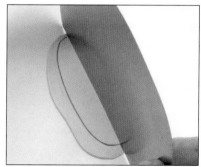

6. Cut lengthwise through the center of the oval shape.

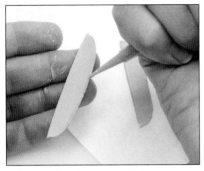

7. Supporting the clay carefully, apply syringe clay to the curved edge of one half of the oval.

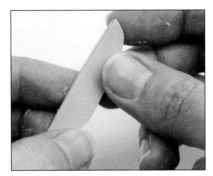

8. Press the second half over the first, carefully aligning the pieces. Hold for a moment.

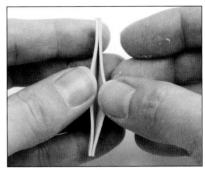

9. Open up the straight sides a bit to begin forming a canoe shape.

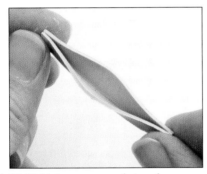

10. Hold the narrow ends together and press them toward the center as you gently work the shape open. (This step reminds me of preparing a baked potato.)

11. Apply a blob of syringe clay in the spot where you plan to set the pearl. Insert the marred end of wire through the syringe blob and into the wet clay at the seam, making sure you don't push it beyond the seam.

Dry and refine
12. Gently set the pearl inside the pod, next to the wire. This will help ensure that the pod will not close up too much as it dries.

13. Set the piece aside to dry completely. Prop it against something like a pencil or shaper tool as shown.

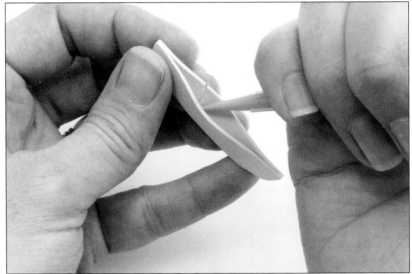

14. Remove the pearl. Apply additional syringe clay to the base of the wire if it seems at all loose.

15. Apply additional syringe clay generously to the outside of the seam.

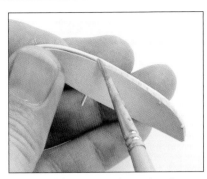

16. Blend the syringe clay with a damp brush. Dry again.

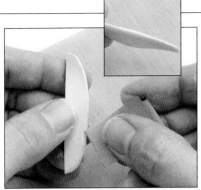

17. Smooth the outside at the seam, holding the sandpaper at a slight angle to taper the edge. Work toward shaping the piece like a real pod, not like two pieces stuck together.

18. Sand the front edges so they also have a taper. Run a damp finger over the outside to smooth any minor sanding scratches.

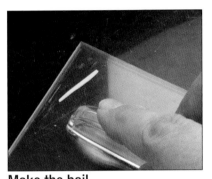

Make the bail
19. Using an ungreased snake roller on an ungreased underlay, roll a very thin snake with the conditioned extra clay.

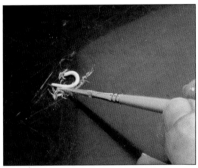

20. Brush lightly with water. Use the brush to bend the snake into a C shape about ⅛" tall for the bail.

21. Trim the ends straight. Dry.

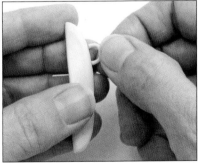

22. Sand the bail to fit along the back of the pod shape near the top of the pendant with both ends on the seam.

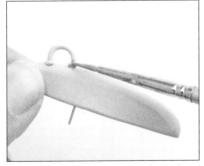

23. Use syringe clay to attach the bail. Smooth the ooze with the brush. Dry. Apply additional syringe clay to the points where the bail meets the pod.

Fire

24. Trim the wire so it does not stick out past the straight edges of the pod. Use a dry paintbrush to thoroughly clean any clay dust from the inside of the pod. Set the pod on a firebrick with the flat edges down (seam side up).

25. Prop with bits of fiber blanket if needed. Fire for 3 minutes. Set aside to cool naturally. (Because this piece has multiple components, you want to avoid thermal shock from quenching.)

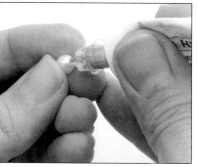

Finish and polish

26. Use a small steel-bristle brush for a scratch finish on the inside of the pendant.

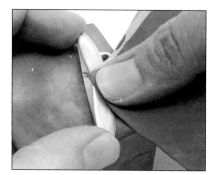

27. On the outside, work through 600-, 1200-, and then 2000-grit wet/dry sandpaper with water to achieve a shiny finish. Finally, rub with a polishing cloth to reveal a brilliant shine.

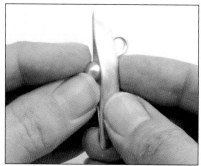

28. Trim the wire to a length that works for the pearl. Rough up the tip of wire with sandpaper. Apply jewelry cement to the hole in the pearl.

29. Press the pearl down firmly onto the wire. Let the cement cure fully according to the manufacturer's directions.

ANOTHER IDEA

Try texturing both sides of the clay by forming disks inside a concave item such as a the round well of a paint palette. Set wires in the wet clay. After the disks are dry, drill holes at the top to accommodate headpins. Set the half-drilled pearls and adorn the headpins with more pearls after firing and polishing.

PROJECT 17
Molded charms

Finished diameter: 1⅛" (largest charm)

WHAT YOU'LL NEED

Basics
- Two-part molding compound
- 10–20 grams Art Clay Silver 650 or PMC+
- 9 6mm jump rings, 18 gauge
- 18" sterling silver chain
- Lobster claw clasp
- Metal clay tool kit

Specialty tools
- 1 large and 3 small buttons or other items to mold
- Inexpensive paintbrush dedicated to use with olive oil
- Fondant tool or clay shaper (optional)
- Drill bit
- Tumbler (optional)

Making molds is fun and rather addictive! Using self-curing molding material makes it almost instant gratification. Just knead the material together and press in an object. Let it cure for a few minutes and it is ready to go. Capture the designs of buttons, doorknobs, antique silverware, and almost anything without damaging the original, and then press in clay to translate the treasure into fine silver.

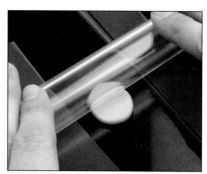

Make a mold

1. For a ½" (small) button, mix a small blob (roughly a blueberry-sized ball) of each color of the molding compound together until it's evenly colored. (Use more compound for a large item.)

2. Roll the compound into a flat disk that is at least 14 cards thick (4 cards thicker than the item being molded).

3. Press the button firmly into the compound. Leave the button in place and set aside to cure flat on a smooth, nonporous surface such as glass. It will cure in about five minutes. To check, press your fingernail into the edge of the mold. If the nail does not leave an impression, it is cured. Make molds of all four items.

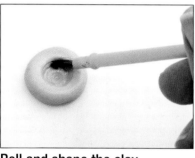

Roll and shape the clay

4. Set up your workspace. Lightly grease any tools and supplies that will touch the clay. Use a paintbrush to apply a light coating of olive oil to all the nooks and crannies of the mold. Blot off any excess oil with a paper towel.

> **TIP** If you are going to sell your work, be sure that whatever you are molding is not copyrighted by the original designer. This goes for rubber stamps as well; many commercial designs are for personal use only, not for resale. Chances are if your item to be molded is antique, it is no longer protected by copyright.

5. For a small charm, roll 5 grams of clay into a disk that is 5 cards thick. Press the clay into the greased mold. Use more clay for a larger item.

6. Working from the middle out, use your fingers, a fondant tool, or a clay shaper to press the clay deep into the design.

7. Gently remove the clay from the mold and place it on a nonstick sheet. Trim the clay about 1mm away from the design with a craft knife. Dry.

8. Repeat with the remaining clay to make two charms from each small mold and one large charm.

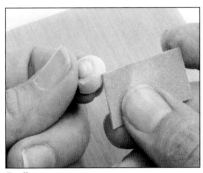

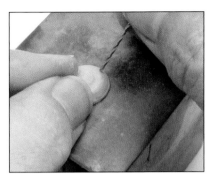

Refine
9. Use 180-grit sandpaper to sand the edges to meet the design of each charm.

10. Use a drill bit to make a hole about 3mm from the edge of each charm.

Fire
11. Place three of the small charms on the firebrick face up and as close together as possible, almost touching. Because the charms are rather thick, fire for 4 minutes. Let the charms cool on the brick for a minute and then quench. Because they are thick, an instant quench could cause a crack. Fire the large charm separately.

Finish and polish
12. Brush with a brass-bristle brush. Because of all the dimension in the charms, the easiest way to make them shiny is to use a tumbler, but you can also polish by hand.

Assemble
13. Assemble into a necklace by connecting the charms to the chain with jump rings. Attach a clasp on one end of the chain with a jump ring.

ANOTHER IDEA

Keep your eyes open
for mold shapes. Sometimes unusual items can lend themselves to molding!

My daughter had a treasure chest toy with the coolest design on the top of the chest. I always liked it, and when I discovered how to make my own molds, I knew that I wanted to make a mold from it.

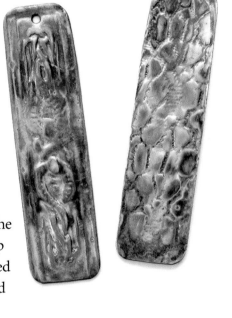

PROJECT18
Mosaic pendant

This pendant came about because my cat jumped up on my work table and broke one of my dry pendants. It was too broken to repair, but I really liked it and did not want to turn it back into soft clay. Months later, my husband saw a mosaic mural and suggested I set those broken pieces like tiles in wet clay mortar. I used each tile as a tiny canvas for a different technique of applying patina. Read through the project before you get started to decide which method you'd like to try.

Finished height: 1½"

WHAT YOU'LL NEED

Basics
- 20 grams Art Clay Silver 650 or PMC+
- Art Clay Silver 650 Paste, or PMC+ Slip
- Art Clay Silver 650 Syringe, green tip, or PMC+ Syringe, pink tip
- Baking soda
- Metal clay tool kit

Specialty tools & supplies
- Rubber stamps with small, deep patterns
- Clear sealant such as Renaissance wax or Krylon Crystal Clear (optional)

Patina method 1
- Liver of sulfur, chunk form
- 2 glass bowls
- Ammonia
- Salt
- 2 candle warmers

Patina method 2
- Liver of sulfur, chunk form
- Cotton swabs
- Toothpicks
- 2 glass bowls
- Ammonia
- Salt
- 2 candle warmers

Patina method 3
- Liver of sulfur, chunk form
- 2 glass bowls
- Coffee
- Ammonia
- Salt
- 2 candle warmers

Patina method 4
- Liver of sulfur, gel form
- Cotton swab

TIP The gel formula of liver of sulfur creates more-vivid rainbow effects than other types (chunk or liquid). You can dilute the gel with water or use it straight out of the bottle—very convenient!

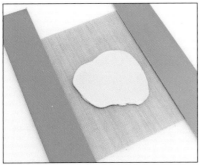

Roll and shape the clay

1. Set up your workspace. If you'd like a guide for trimming the clay, copy the pattern and place it under the nonstick sheet. Lightly grease any tools and supplies that will touch the clay. Working quickly, roll out a third of the clay to 3 cards thick.

2. Place the clay on the greased stamp. Set 2-card-thick slats or stacks on the stamp on both sides of the clay. Texture the clay with one firm roll.

3. Use a cutter to trim the shape. Wrap the bail projection around a greased straw to create a rolled bail.

4. Apply syringe clay along the seam to seal the bail. Smooth with a moist brush.

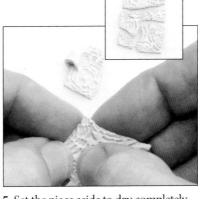

5. Set the piece aside to dry completely. Sand the edges, then break the clay into five pieces. Set the pieces aside.

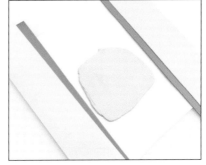

6. Condition and moisturize the remaining clay to be rather wet, but not sticky. Roll it to 5 cards thick and about ¼" taller and wider than the original pendant. (You can check the size against the pattern copy.)

pattern

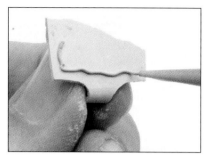

7. Working quickly, apply syringe clay to the back of the broken piece that includes the bail. Set it in place near the top of the piece of wet clay.

8. Place the remaining pieces in the same way, always setting the next nearest "tile" with a small gap between them until all the remaining pieces are used. Press each piece firmly into the wet clay until the clay is squeezed up like grout between the pieces.

9. Trim the edges, leaving a border at least as wide as the grout. Dry and sand.

Fire
10. This piece is rather thick, so be sure that it is completely dry before firing. Fire for 4 minutes. Set aside to cool naturally.

Finish
11. Brush the entire piece with the brass-bristle brush. Use different finishing techniques on each tile, from scratch-finishing to burnishing, to get the best variety of effects with liver of sulfur solution. Shiny silver is more likely to produce rainbow colors. Wash the pendant with warm, soapy water. Dry.

ANOTHER IDEA

Make a leaf mosaic pendant by using a cookie cutter to
make the first shape. Attach a bail after the pendant is dry. I left this pendant as it looked after firing, with its white surface of unburnished silver.

Add patina
12. Working in a well-ventilated area, use a liver of sulfur solution to enhance texture and add color to the piece.

Choose among the following methods for this step:

Method 1: dip
This is the easiest method because the reaction is slow and you have lots of control. The down side is that all of the tiles might end up looking the same. The finish variations you created will help make each piece look different.

Dissolve a small chunk of LOS in a small bowl filled with warm water. (The hotter the water, the quicker the reaction; don't make it too hot or you may not be able to catch the color at the stage you like.) Add ½ tablespoon of ammonia

and ½ teaspoon of salt. Place the bowl on a mug warmer. Fill another small bowl with warm water and place it on the second mug warmer. Fill a third bowl with cold water.

Hold the pendant with a pair of tweezers so you can easily see the design side and don't let go of it throughout this process. Dunk the piece into the warm water first. Hold it there for a few seconds to preheat the piece, then do a super-quick dip in the LOS solution, then swish it around a bit in the cold water. Continue dipping in this way, observing the changes, until you like the patina on the pendant.

The shinier the silver is, the more likely it is to take on a dramatic color with liver of sulfur.

Method 2: painting

I love the control of using a cotton swab to add color to very specific areas. Prepare the LOS solution as in Method 1. Holding the pendant with tweezers, dip it into warm water first. Saturate a cotton swab with the LOS solution or pick up a drop with a toothpick. Paint it onto one tile at a time. When the desired effect is reached, transfer the pendant to the cold water. You can re-apply to the same area to bring out more color. Repeat to color each tile.

Method 3: coffee dip

Sometimes using coffee as a base can give you really nice colors. Replace the warm water in Method 1 with warm coffee. The rest of the technique is the same as Method 1.

Use a polishing pad or cloth to remove patina from selected areas (such as the bail or grout) if desired. Don't polish the tiles—it will diminish the colors.

Method 4: undiluted gel

This is my new favorite way to add patina! I like it because you don't have to get out a bunch of bowls and it is not as smelly.

Have a cotton swab and a bottle of gel patina handy near a source for hot, running water. Apply some gel to a dry cotton swab. Paint it on one tile.

Hold the piece under the hot running water face down. Keep it there for a few seconds and then check the color. If the color has not developed enough, either hold it face down under the water for a few seconds or apply more gel first.

TIP This undiluted method works because the gel is already dissolved, so you can apply it straight out of the bottle. Holding it under the hot running water upside-down will heat the metal without washing off the patina. The heated piece will then develop color faster.

For all methods, rinse thoroughly under running water and soak in a bowl of water with a teaspoon of dissolved baking soda. This will help neutralize the LOS and prevent it from continuing to affect the silver. Dry.

Seal

You have the option at this point of sealing the silver to help preserve the patina. There are several options, including Renaissance wax, which creates a soft finish. To use it, apply a bit with a soft cloth. Let it dry, then buff with a clean, soft cloth.

A spray coating such as Krylon Crystal Clear will leave a shinier finish. Be sure to apply several light coats instead of one heavy coat. Use it outside because it is not good to breathe the vapors. Any sealant will slightly alter the look of the patina, but it will help maintain the color for a very long time.

PROJECT **19**

Paper overlay pendant

Paper-type clay, also called sheet clay, is really fun to work with. It behaves a lot like regular paper. You can cut it with fancy scissors, emboss it, fold it, and more. For this project, you'll use paper punches to cut out wonderful little decorative shapes and then apply them to textured clay to make a pendant with lots of details.

Finished size: 1⅞"

WHAT YOU'LL NEED

Basics
- 20 grams Art Clay Silver 650 or PMC+
- Art Clay Silver 650 Paste or PMC+ Slip
- Art Clay Silver Paper Type or PMC+ Sheet
- Art Clay Silver Syringe, green tip, or PMC+ Syringe, pink tip
- Metal clay tool kit

Specialty tools & supplies
- Freezer paper
- Small decorative paper punches
- Large rubber stamp or stamp sheet
- Lace or netting swatches
- 1.5mm drill bit (#53)
- 1" and 2" leaf-shaped cutters
- Smooth-jaw pliers
- Pointed-tip clay shaper
- Large sanding swabs (optional)

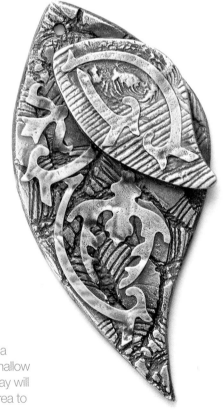

TIP

For this project, select a rubber stamp with a shallow design so the paper clay will have a large surface area to connect with.

Shape the base

1. Set up your workspace. Lightly grease any tools and supplies that will touch the clay, including the plastic-coated side of the freezer paper. On the freezer paper, roll 15 grams of clay 4 cards thick. Place the lace on top of clay and roll again at 4 cards thick, keeping the texture between (not on top of) the slats or stacks. Peel off the lace.

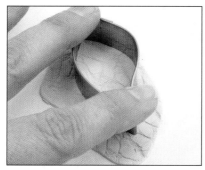

2. Cut the clay with the large leaf-shaped cutter. Use the drill bit to make a hole at the top.

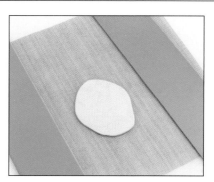

3. Roll the remaining 5 grams of clay to 3 cards thick. Transfer to a greased rubber stamp.

4. Place 2-card-thick slats or stacks on both sides of the clay, on top of the stamp. Roll firmly once over the clay to texture it.

5. Use the small leaf-shaped cutter to cut out a small leaf. Dry the leaf shapes.

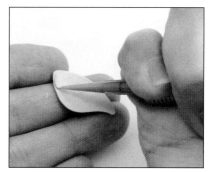

6. Sand the edges of each leaf. Apply a bead of syringe clay along the edge of the back of the small leaf.

7. Place on the large leaf as shown and press down.

8. Use a moist brush to smooth the ooze. Dry thoroughly. Sand again.

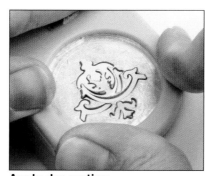

Apply decoration

9. Use paper punches to punch shapes from the paper clay. You can use the punch upside down to position the clay and minimize waste.

Tips for working with paper clay

- Too much water will make the paper disintegrate.
- Heat will cause the paper to become brittle and crack.
- Paste will damage the pristine visible surface of the paper, so be sure that no ooze gets on top.
- Apply paper clay to regular clay if you want to torch-fire the piece; it isn't sturdy enough to be fired by itself.

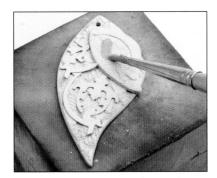

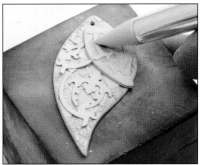

10. Thin a small amount of paste clay with water until it is the consistency of cream. Brush a small amount of thinned paste onto an area of the pendant slightly larger than the punched shape.

11. Using smooth-jaw tweezers, position the appliqué pieces. There must be some paste under all parts of the appliqué.

12. Use the clay shaper to press the appliqués in place. Wipe the shaper often to keep the paste off the appliqué shapes. Set aside to dry at room temperature for 10–20 minutes. Flip the pendant over and decorate the back with additional paper appliqués. Set aside to dry without heat.

Fire

13. Set the piece on the firebrick. Fire for 4 minutes. Cool naturally. Do not quench.

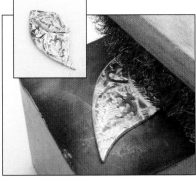

Finish and polish

14. Be careful when finishing the piece; you don't want to chip off any of the appliqué work. I recommend simply brushing gently with a brass brush. The paper has a smooth surface that contrasts beautifully with the textured clay beneath.

15. Enhance the texture with a dip in a liver of sulfur solution.

16. Rinse, dry, and rub with the polishing cloth to restore the highlights.

ANOTHER IDEA

These paper overlay beads

make great focal pieces. Texture the clay on one side only and form it as though you are making a really skinny ring around a straw. You can add a skinny snake border on the top and bottom if you like. The paper clay is flexible enough to wrap around the bead.

PROJECT 20

Copper clay pendant

Finished width: 1⅞"

WHAT YOU'LL NEED

Basics
- 15 grams Art Clay Copper (do not substitute other brands of copper clay or use bronze clay)
- Freezer paper
- Copper clay tool kit

Specialty tools
- Rubber stamp with deep texture
- Soda can or other large cylinder
- Fiber blanket
- 2 pairs of tweezers
- Quenching bowl, medium sized
- Needle tool
- Pickle pot
- Citric acid or Sparex
- Copper tweezers
- Tumbler (optional)
- Steel bench block

Now that you're comfortable working with silver clay, try copper! It requires a few additional tools and techniques, but the lower cost of the clay itself can make up for the extra investment if you like this metal. You can achieve a beautiful color spectrum with a heat patina that is unique to copper.

TIP

Be cautious about the brand you choose for this project. At the time of publication, Art Clay Copper was the only brand of base-metal clay that can be successfully torch-fired. Other copper and bronze clays on the market require a kiln and a pan filled with carbon to fire. Don't be tempted to try torch-firing the other types! The pieces will crumble into dust.

Copper clay basics

Working with wet clay

It's a good idea to have a set of basic wet-working tools for base metal clays, including copper clay, that you keep separate from your silver clay tools. Copper residue can prevent the silver clay from sintering properly. At a minimum, have duplicates of the items that directly touch wet clay, such as work surfaces and rollers, as well as files and sandpaper. Thoroughly clean any other items that might transfer residue or clay dust.

You can do a really good job of cleaning some tools like rollers if you choose not to invest in duplicate items. Some things must be duplicated because they are impossible to clean well enough like paintbrushes, sandpaper, and files. Be very careful with rubber stamps. If you want to use them for silver later, give them a good scrubbing with soapy water and a baby toothbrush.

Here are a few of the ways in which copper clay is different from silver clay:

- It doesn't adhere to itself as easily as silver clay does
- Sometimes copper clay can be a little stiff right out of the package; it may need to be conditioned with a bit of water even when new
- You must work thicker
- It does not come in paste or syringe form
- It takes more time and/or heat to dry
- It must be pickled (soaked in an acidic solution) after firing because the copper oxidizes and turns black
- It is much less expensive than silver

Copper clay storage

Once opened, copper clay does not keep as long as silver clay. Store it by wrapping clay tightly in plastic wrap and sealing it in a small zip-top bag. Wrap it in wet paper towels and then wrap in aluminum foil. It will last for a couple of weeks or so as long as it stays moist. It does not need to be refrigerated. Don't worry if you see small amounts of oxidation on the surface (brown spots). Just blend it all together while conditioning.

Copper dust is not worth keeping as it can not be turned back into clay.

At publication time, copper clay was not available in paste or syringe form. If you want to connect copper clay together, you must make up a little batch of paste yourself by mashing a bit of clay and water together with a palette knife. Because copper clay does not adhere to itself well, always use some paste as well as pressure and a shaping tool to press the layers into each other.

Firing copper clay

Copper clay loses several card thicknesses during the processes of firing, quenching, and pickling. Because of this, be sure to make all pieces thicker than usual, and even more so if the piece will be kiln-fired. Because so much surface material will be lost, all textures must be rather deep to remain intact.

Because you will roll copper clay thicker than silver, allow about 25% extra drying time. Art Clay Copper shrinks 10%, and it is the only copper clay currently sold that can be successfully torch-fired.

The desired color during firing is a cherry red, not the peach color you look for with silver. The firing time is longer: 7+ minutes for a 25-gram piece. After firing, the copper will be covered with

black firescale (undesirable oxidation). Quickly pick up the firebrick and dump the hot piece into a stainless steel bowl filled with cold water. The thermal shock of the cold will cause most of the firescale to pop off. (If you do not put it in water, as it cools, tiny bits of oxidation will begin popping off and shooting around the room.) Leave the piece in the water a few minutes to help get off as much as possible. Use a sharp tool to help pick off any loose bits of firescale.

Pickling setup

You'll need a vessel to hold an acidic solution that will remove the black firescale that accumulates on copper clay pieces when they are fired. This "pickle" is the same process jewelers use for cleaning sterling silver. Once used for pickle, do not use the container for anything else. Miniature electric crocks are easy to find and heat to the perfect temperature. I like to use a less-caustic pickling solution of citric acid (available at health food stores) and water instead of the traditional Sparex solution.

Use long copper tweezers to transfer the piece to the pickle pot. Let it soak in the pickle until it is clean. Be sure not to leave copper in the pickle for too long or it will begin to pit. Never touch the pickle solution—it is an acid. Use the copper tweezers to remove the piece from the pickle and transfer it to a bowl of fresh water. Dry. You can use LOS on copper pieces as well.

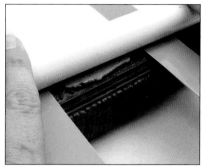

Roll and shape the clay

1. Set up your workspace. Lightly grease any tools and supplies that will touch the clay, including the plastic-coated side of the freezer paper. Tape the freezer paper to the soda can and squash the bottom of the can a bit so it will not roll when placed in its side. Set aside.

Open the clay and add a bit of water to condition the clay if it seems dry. Roll all of the clay to 7 cards thick.

2. Transfer the clay to a rubber stamp and texture it at 5 cards thick.

3. Curve the cutter/scraper to trim the top as shown. Trim the sides straight.

 TIP The difference between the rolling and texturing thicknesses is greater than usual because the design needs to be very deep to remain visible after firing and pickling.

4. Pick up the clay and, starting at one side, tear the bottom edge at an angle. To tear, pinch the clay along the edge and gently pull the excess toward you. Continue pinching and pulling all the way across to the other side.

5. Make two holes near the upper corners with a straw, making sure that the holes are at least one straw's-width away from each edge.

6. Drape the clay shape over the prepared can. Dry.

ANOTHER IDEA

Try making a textured band with copper clay. Use an embeddable copper finding and stone to add sparkle. Art Clay Copper shrinks about 10% and the ring will get a bit bigger when metal is lost due to firescale, so for a ¼"-wide band, work about a size larger than the desired finished size to compensate. Make your own paste to seal the seam. Re-create texture across the seam or smooth it if there is no texture. Press the setting into a blob of paste on top of the seam and smooth to help disguise the seam and hold it together at the same time!

Refine the shape
7. Lightly sand the edges. Smooth any sharp points on the torn edge.

Fire
8. Support the piece well with a piece of fiber blanket on the firebrick. (Remember to wash your hands after touching the fiber.)

9. Make sure your torch is fully fueled; copper clay takes a long time and needs a higher temperature than silver to sinter. Bring the piece up to a deep cherry red color and start the timer. Hold at that color for 8 minutes. You don't need to worry as much about melting the clay because copper has a much higher melting point than silver.

10. Immediately after you remove the flame, the piece will turn black. This surface oxidation is called firescale; to remove it, you need to quench the piece quickly after firing.

11. Hold a pair of tweezers in each hand. With one pair, hold the fiber blanket down as it is going to want to stick to the fired copper. With the other pair, pick up the pendant and drop it quickly into the quenching bowl filled with plenty of water. Instantly, most of the firescale will pop off the surface.

Finish
12. There may still be some big bits of black that should be removed to make pickling easier. Use a needle tool or other sharp point to pick out these big pieces. Don't worry about little things and blotches; the pickle will take care of those.

Mix up a batch of pickle according to the manufacturer's directions and warm it in the pickle pot. Heat the solution in a well-ventilated area to prevent breathing any fumes.

TIP

Use caution around pickle. Wear old clothes or an apron as you use it and never put your hands in it—it is an acid and will burn skin and make holes in clothing.

Citric acid, found at health-food stores, makes a less-caustic pickle solution. Place two cups of water into a small electric crock pot. Add ¼ cup citric acid to the water. Stir with copper tongs; never use stainless steel in pickle. Plug in the pot. A hot solution works best.

13. When the pickle solution is hot, use copper tweezers to place the piece into the pickle pot. Let it soak in the solution until the firescale is gone. This could vary from 3–30 minutes depending on the type of solution you are using (Sparex is fast; citric acid is slow). Do not leave in the pickle solution much beyond 30 minutes or the copper will pit. Rinse and dry.

14. Brush with a brass brush. The copper will have a soft golden sheen after brushing. You can stop here if you like this look.

15. If you want to add some color to the piece, try creating a heat patina using the butane torch. This works best if the surface has been burnished or the piece has been tumbled to a shiny, almost pink color.

16. Place the steel block on the firebrick. With tweezers, hold most of the piece over the block with just a bit projecting over the edge. Turn on the torch, apply heat gingerly to the overhanging edge, and watch the color begin to develop. If you notice a bit of condensation on the block, don't worry.

17. The piece will turn light orange.

18. It will change to hot pink and possibly an icy blue. Continue heating until the desired color is reached, and then quickly slide the piece back onto the steel block to cool it and stop the color from progressing. Let it continue to cool on the block; quenching will alter the patina.

Are you ready for more?

I'm offering this slightly advanced information for readers who have tried a few of the simpler projects in this book and are ready to take their knowledge a little further. I hope you've gotten your hands a little dirty and are ready to learn a few intermediate bonus tips to help you enjoy more success in making metal clay jewelry.

Construction considerations

Keep in mind that there are different ways of working with metals, and each has its own benefits.

Using metal clay is a time- and cost-efficient way to create complex shapes. The resulting sintered metals are strong, but not very flexible.

You would not want to make and fire a cuff bracelet flat, then hammer it into a curved shape. Likewise, you would not want to resize a ring by putting it on a ring mandrel and smacking it with a hammer; it will break.

Imagine all of those tiny silver particles that are connected to each other at particular points. When you bend the piece, you would be breaking those connections.

Take advantage of the clay state to shape things as you would like them, then dry and fire in that shape for a sturdy outcome. There are exceptions to this—ways of kiln-firing that would make a silver clay piece flexible enough to reshape—however, those methods are beyond the scope of this book. You may enjoy taking classes to learn more about advanced ways of working with metal clay.

Making connections

Choose among these connection techniques based on the state of each piece to be connected. I have found that the methods vary slightly for each brand of clay.

Regardless of method or brand, dry the pieces fully after connecting them, and then check to see if you need to reinforce anywhere.

Wet/wet with ACS
Apply a layer of paste to the smaller of the two pieces to be assembled. Set it in position, press the pieces together, and hold for 3 seconds.

Wet/dry with ACS
Apply some water to the connecting surface of the dry piece. Let it soak in, then apply paste or syringe. Immediately press the pieces together. Hold for 3 seconds. Smooth the ooze with a moist brush.

Dry/dry with ACS
Apply some water to the connecting surfaces of each piece. Let it soak in. Apply a bit more water to one of the surfaces, and then apply a bead of syringe to the same piece. Press

the pieces together and hold for 3 seconds. Smooth the ooze with a moist brush.

Wet/wet with PMC
Moisten the smaller of the pieces to be assembled with some water. Set it in position, and then press the pieces together and hold for 3 seconds. This is an especially easy method with PMC. It really grabs onto itself.

Wet/dry with PMC
Apply some water to the connecting surface of the dry piece. Let it soak in, and then add another bit of water. Immediately press the pieces together. Hold for 3 seconds.

Dry/dry with PMC
Apply some water to the connecting surfaces of each piece. Let it soak in. Apply a bit more water to one of the surfaces, and then apply a generous amount of slip to the same piece. Press the pieces together and hold for 3 seconds. Smooth the ooze with a moist brush.

Reconditioning clay

To recondition leftover clay, gather the scraps in a square of plastic wrap and add a drop of water. Fold the plastic over and squash the clay with your thumb until it is flat [**A**], and squash again. Always begin pushing near the fold and work toward the edges to ensure you don't trap air pockets that will cause big problems later. Keep folding, turning, and squashing [**B**].

Do this at least five times and check the consistency (see below) before you decide whether to add more water. It takes at least five turns for the water to fully incorporate into the clay. If you add water more quickly, the clay will likely suddenly turn to mush. In most situations, clay can be ready to use again in minutes. Even totally dry clay can be reconditioned!

Perfect!

The clay should have a perfectly smooth texture—totally free of lumps. It should yield to the touch when you push on it. If it takes any force to put a thumb-mark in it, add more water. The result will resemble Silly Putty.

Needs more water

If the clay is really stiff and unyielding, it needs more water. Another sign would be that the edges crack as you press down. Add another drop or two of water and work it in with at least five turns. Assess and repeat as necessary.

Needs more squashing

Lumps do not equal "needs more water"! This is the number-one mistake people make when conditioning clay. If you have soft clay that is full of lumps or looks like oatmeal, you need to squash a lot more. Press the clay really firmly against a table to help crush the lump. Once it is crushed, it will easily incorporate in the clay. After the lumps are gone, check the overall consistency and add water as needed.

Too wet

It is easy to recognize clay that is too wet. It will stick all over the plastic wrap and your finger will push through it easily. This one takes a bit of time to fix because the excess water needs some time to evaporate. Lightly fold the plastic over and set aside for several hours to overnight. Do a few turns and repeat as necessary. This may create some crispies in the clay that will put you in the "needs more squashing" category.

Totally dry

If the clay is totally dry or you want to destroy an unfired piece, break up the dry clay into the smallest pieces possible into a piece of plastic wrap. Add several drops of water, wrap tightly, and set aside until the next day in a moist environment. Open the plastic, fold it over the clay, and start squashing.

Check the consistency; you will most likely need to add a few more drops of water. If the chunks are still rather large, set the clay aside for several more hours. After it sits for a while, you should be able to treat it like fresh clay.

TIP Never try to use a rubber stamp to texture clay that is too wet. It will smear and stick mercilessly.

Reclaiming clay

There are always leftovers and mistakes, and that's OK. In any case, we do not want to waste silver! Here are a few ways to save the day.

Dust to paste

This is perhaps the easiest way to reclaim clay. Simply gather up the silver dust, dump it into the paste/slip jar, add a few drops of water, and stir a bit. By the next day, it will be ready to go.

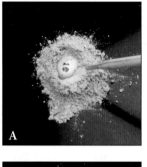

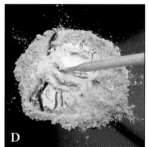

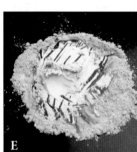

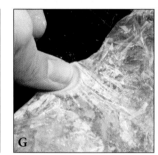

Dust to clay

If you do a lot of sanding or filing, you will have lots of silver dust. Perhaps you have no need for that amount of paste. Instead, make more clay! Keep in mind that any gunk in the dust will be gunk in the clay, so use pure dust. Place the dust on a smooth work surface and make a well in the middle. Add a few drops of distilled water to the well [A]. Use a palette knife to begin working the water into the dust [B, C]. Gradually add more water to incorporate more dust [D]. Continue until most of the dust is used [E]. Transfer to a piece of plastic wrap [F] and work in the last dust as you would water: fold, squash, fold, squash, repeat [G]. Let it sit overnight and work it inside the plastic a few more times. Check the consistency and make adjustments to the water content if necessary [H].

Reclaiming clay (continued)

Clay to clay

When a piece of clay does not roll or texture well, dab off the excess oil and gather up the clay. Place it in a piece of plastic wrap with a drop of water. Knead the water into the clay (see "Reconditioning," p. 107). Even if the clay has been out only a few minutes, the surface has begun to dry and it will have a hard time coming together as perfectly smooth clay again. Taking a moment to condition the clay will help ensure the best finished pieces.

Dry to clay

Say you have some pieces that have not been fired yet and you just don't really care for them anymore. Or perhaps you have some clay that accidentally got left out for a month in the middle of summer. Don't worry! These can be turned back into clay. On a piece of plastic wrap, break up the dry clay into the smallest pieces possible. Add several drops of water, wrap tightly, and set aside until the next day in a moist environment.

The next day, open the plastic, fold it over the clay, and start squashing. Check the consistency; you will most likely need to add a few drops more water. If the chunks are still rather large set aside for several more hours. By now, you should be able to condition it as you would regular clay.

Fixing wet mistakes

When something happens to wet clay, it's a really good time to decide whether you would be better off starting over again. In many circumstances, you will save time in the end by reconditioning the clay and remaking the piece. There are some exceptions because these are easy-to-repair boo-boos (below).

Holes/fingernail marks

Just to be sure no additional misfortunes happen to a piece, let it dry before attempting any repairs. Moisten the flawed area and overfill with syringe clay or tiny bits of wet clay. Dry and sand.

Hair/pet fur

It always comes as a surprise to find a bit of Fluffy's fur embedded in your clay. Wait until the clay is dry, and then use a pair of tweezers to pick out the hair. If it is small, lightly sand the area with 2000-grit sandpaper. If it is large, use some paste to fill, dry, and sand.

Bad shape

Certainly do not remake something if the shape did not come out just right. Wait until it's dry and then reshape with sandpaper. If you need to make something a lot smaller, use a jeweler's saw to cut it down once dry. You will be surprised to see how easy metal clay is to saw!

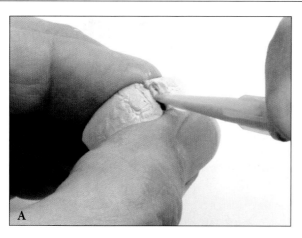

Repairing broken pieces

Dry break

If the project has broken into more than three pieces, start over and make clay out of the broken bits (see "Salvaging: Dry to Clay").

If your piece has broken into just three or fewer pieces, arrange the pieces so you know how to put them back together again (metal clay typically breaks into pieces that fit together perfectly like a jigsaw puzzle).

Repairing a dry break is a three-step process. If you leave out a step, your work will break again!

1. Moisten two matching broken edges and apply a bead of syringe clay to one of the edges [**A**]. Set both pieces on a piece of nonstick sheet. Press the two pieces firmly together and hold for three seconds. Use a moist paintbrush to smooth the ooze that appears on the front surface. Try to keep the excess clay by blending it in with the surrounding design. You should not be able to see anything from the front. Dry.

2. Flip the piece over. Wet the seam area. Let it soak in a bit, then apply more syringe along the break [**B**]. Use a moist brush to blend the ooze. Leave it mounded up a bit. Dry.

3. Lightly sand the mound on the back side. The idea here is to remove most of the syringe clay, but leave a very well-blended (invisible) bridge of clay that spans the break. If you sand it all off, the piece will likely break again in the exact same place.

Fired break

This can happen if a piece of metal clay is underfired or stressed. Improperly sintered metal will be very brittle. If it's smacked or dropped, it can break.

Try to avoid polishing a broken edge because it is easier for the metal to adhere to itself after firing with the naturally rough, crystalline edge.

The product to use to fix a fired break is Art Clay Silver Overlay Paste. Ordinary paste lacks the special ingredients that allow it to bond to fired silver. (Art Clay Silver Oil Paste is specifically designed for this purpose, but it must be kiln-fired; if you have a kiln, you have a few other options as well.)

Apply a generous layer of the overlay paste. Smooth the ooze a bit and then dry. Do not try to sand before firing. The sandpaper will get gummed up and the piece will likely break again from all the fiddling. Refire and then use metal files to grind off any uglies. Sand and polish as usual.

Another option is to save up fired mistakes and send them to a metal refinery. Many places will buy silver by weight to recycle.

About the author

Cindy Thomas Pankopf is a teacher and author who's passionate about sharing her knowledge of metal clay. Through her books and in-person instruction, she inspires and challenges her students to develop their technical skills and artistry. She has a true gift for helping beginning students feel comfortable with the medium and also finds it rewarding to teach certification classes to others, so they in turn have the skills and credentials to guide others.

Cindy's beadwork and metal clay designs have won awards and have been featured in many publications. She has attained the master level of instructor certification with Art Clay World, is certified in PMC, and was the charter president of the Art Clay Society of Orange County. She enjoys teaching at Milwaukee's Bead&Button Show, BABE!, and other national venues, and holds workshops in her Fullerton, California, studio as well. Cindy has a B.S. degree in Applied Art and Design from California Polytechnic State University, San Luis Obispo, and worked as a graphic designer for 15 years before turning her professional life over to metal clay and jewelry making. She is the author of *Beadmaille: Jewelry with Bead Weaving and Metal Rings*, a book that features her hybrid style of combining seed beads and jump rings into jewelry. Her website is cindypankopf.com.

Technique index

If you'd like to read about certain topics or practice certain techniques, use this index to quickly find popular subjects.

Technique	Project number(s)
Burnishing	4
Draping/forming clay	5, 10, 12, 13, 14, 16, 17
Drilling	5, 7, 8, 9, 11, 12, 16, 17, 19
Dry assembly	11, 12, 19
Embedding findings/wire	6, 15, 16
Molding	17
Paper clay	19
Paste	15, 19
Patinas	1, 3, 9, 11, 12, 18, 19
Rings	13, 14
Rolled bail	4, 5, 18
Satin finish	1, 3, 6, 7, 8, 9, 11, 15, 19
Scratch finish	3, 12, 16
Shiny finish	10, 11, 12, 13, 14, 17
Snakes	6, 8, 13, 14, 15, 16, 19
Stone-setting	6, 7, 8, 16
Syringe clay	4, 5, 7, 8, 9, 10, 11, 12, 18, 19
Templates	3, 10, 11, 16, 18
Texturing	1, 3, 4, 5, 7, 8, 9, 11, 12, 18, 19
Torch-firing	All projects

Acknowledgments

I dedicate this book to Gordon Uyehara, who certified me at level 1 and the senior level for Art Clay. Gordon's grace and ease with metal clay allowed my creativity to blossom, and his influence is apparent to this day in my aesthetic and attention to detail.

Thank you to my wonderful husband, Mike—you always stand by me and my lofty aspirations. And to my children, Keely and Connor—you can do anything you put your mind to! Carol, your decades of support and understanding are invaluable to me. MaryLou, thank you for reviewing new project instructions and helping me prepare for all those process photos. And to my angel Karin, you have no idea how much I rely on your friendship and help. Shannon, my new friend, you are such a fabulous person—I appreciate your help in making my studio space a reality. Stephanie, I am so grateful that you have let me suck you into my world. To my loyal students—thank you for sticking with me through the years.

Thanks to Katie and Patrik for reviewing my product information, and to everyone at Art Clay World USA for all of your support. I am grateful to the team at Kalmbach Books, particularly Mary Wohlgemuth and Lisa Bergman, for making it all come together. And finally, to all my family and friends, thank you for putting up with me as I created a second book on the heels of the first.